Jacob

Whom I Have Chosen, Descendant of Abraham My Friend

Jacob

Whom I Have Chosen, Descendant of Abraham My Friend

Dr. Jaerock Lee

Jacob Whom I Have Chosen, Descendant of Abraham My Friend
by Dr. Jaerock Lee
Published by Urim Books (Representative: Kyungtae Noh)
73, Yeouidaebang-ro 22-gil, Dongjak-Gu, Seoul, Korea
www.urimbooks.com

All rights reserved. This book or parts thereof may not be reproduced in any form, stored in a retrieval system, or transmitted in any form or by any means, electronic, mechanical, photocopying, recording or otherwise, without prior written permission of the publisher.

Unless otherwise noted, all Scripture quotations are taken from the Holy Bible, NEW AMERICAN STANDARD BIBLE, ®, Copyright © 1960, 1962, 1963, 1968, 1971, 1972, 1973, 1975, 1977, 1995 by The Lockman Foundation. Used by permission.

Copyright © 2018 by Dr. Jaerock Lee
ISBN: 979-11-263-0413-4 04230
ISBN: 979-11-263-0412-7 (set)
Translation Copyright © 2016 by Dr. Esther K. Chung. Used by permission.

First Published in June 2018

Previously published in Korean by Urim Books, Seoul, Korea in 2015

Edited by Dr. Geumsun Vin
Designed by Editorial Bureau of Urim Books
Printed by Prione Printing
For more information contact at urimbook@hotmail.com

The earnestness that moved God's heart!
Jacob becomes Israel when he laid himself down!

"But you, Israel, My servant,
Jacob whom I have chosen,
descendant of Abraham My friend,
you whom I have taken from the ends of the earth,
and called from its remotest parts and said to you,
'You are My servant, I have chosen you and not rejected you.
Do not fear, for I am with you;
do not anxiously look about you, for I am your God.
I will strengthen you, surely I will help you,
surely I will uphold you with My righteous right hand.'"

Isaiah 41:8-10

· Words on Publication ·

Jacob Whom I Have Chosen, Descendant of Abraham My Friend

"But now, thus says the LORD, your Creator, O Jacob, and He who formed you, O Israel, Do not fear, for I have redeemed you; I have called you by name; you are Mine!" (Isaiah 43:1)

This is a promise of God that contains His earnest love for Israel, which was formed through Jacob and his children. God planned to establish Jacob as the father of Israel, and for this plan to be fulfilled, Jacob had to go through trials for a long time.

He had good attributes to achieve his goal with an unchanging heart. He had faithfulness and unwavering willpower. However, Jacob had a cunning nature. He relied on his own wisdom and tried to achieve things in his own ways. For this reason he had to go through trials until he became 'Jacob the worm'.

He had to leave his home to run from his angry brother Esau. Esau was angry because Jacob had taken away the blessings for the first son. He even wanted to kill Jacob. So, for more than 20 years, like a slave Jacob had to serve for his uncle Laban, who was crafty and stingy. He could lay down everything only in a stalemate on his way back home.

He clung to God all night long at the River Jabbok and broke himself down completely. And God gave him a new name 'Israel'. He received an amazing blessing; the 12 tribes of Israel were formed through his 12 sons.

This book explains the details of the tumultuous life of Jacob beginning with his birth until Verez was born through his fourth son Judah, who carried on the orthodox genealogy of Abraham. It also explains why Esau couldn't receive the blessing for the first son; why Jacob's fourth son Judah had the birthright; and why Joseph was sold into Egypt as a slave. It contains the deep and mysterious providence of God in these events.

It also explains the spiritual meaning of the names of the 12 tribes of Israel; the differences between the 12 sons of Jacob and the 12 tribes of Israel; and the differences between the 12 disciples of Jesus and the 12 apostles of the Lord after His resurrection.

Israel, which was formed through Jacob's 12 sons, serves as the model of human cultivation as God's elect. But because they eventually forsook the love of God and did not obey Him, the gospel was handed over to the Gentiles. This is also the love of God who wants to save not just the elect Israel but all other peoples as well.

Romans 11:17 says, *"But if some of the branches were broken off, and you, being a wild olive, were grafted in among them and became partaker with them of the rich root of the olive tree."* Here, the olive tree refers to Israel the elect, and the wild olive refers to the Gentiles.

Namely, instead of Israel that denied Jesus and crucified Him, there will be many among the Gentiles that will be saved through Jesus Christ. This providence is embedded in the fact that from among the 12 tribes of Israel, the tribe of Dan was replaced by Manasseh, and from among the 12 disciples of Jesus, Judas Iscariot was replaced by Mathias. The shadow of the Old Testament and the actual substance of the New Testament become a 'mate'.

This is not the end of God's love. After the second coming of the Lord in the air, God allows the 'gleaning salvation' to take place through the 144,000 preachers who come out from the 12 tribes of Israel (Revelation 7:4). It's the love of God who wants to save even just one more soul.

In Revelation chapter 21, we read that, on the 12 Pearl Gates of the city of New Jerusalem are written the names of the 12 tribes, and on the 12 foundation stones are written the names of the 12 apostles. This means that if God's children who have been saved by faith cultivate holiness through obedience and fulfill all their duties, they will be qualified to enter the city of New Jerusalem, which is filled with God's glory.

The faithful love of God the Trinity was given in the Old Testament and will continue to be given to us until the Lord comes back. Through this book I hope the readers will understand this love of God and press on towards the city of New Jerusalem, which is the most beautiful dwelling place in Heaven.

I give thanks to senior deaconess Geumsun Vin, the director of the editorial bureau, her staff, and the staff of Urim Books, and I give all thanks and glory to God the Father who guided us with delicate love.

April 2016,

Jaerock Lee

Abraham's Orthodox Genealogy and Jacob's 12 sons

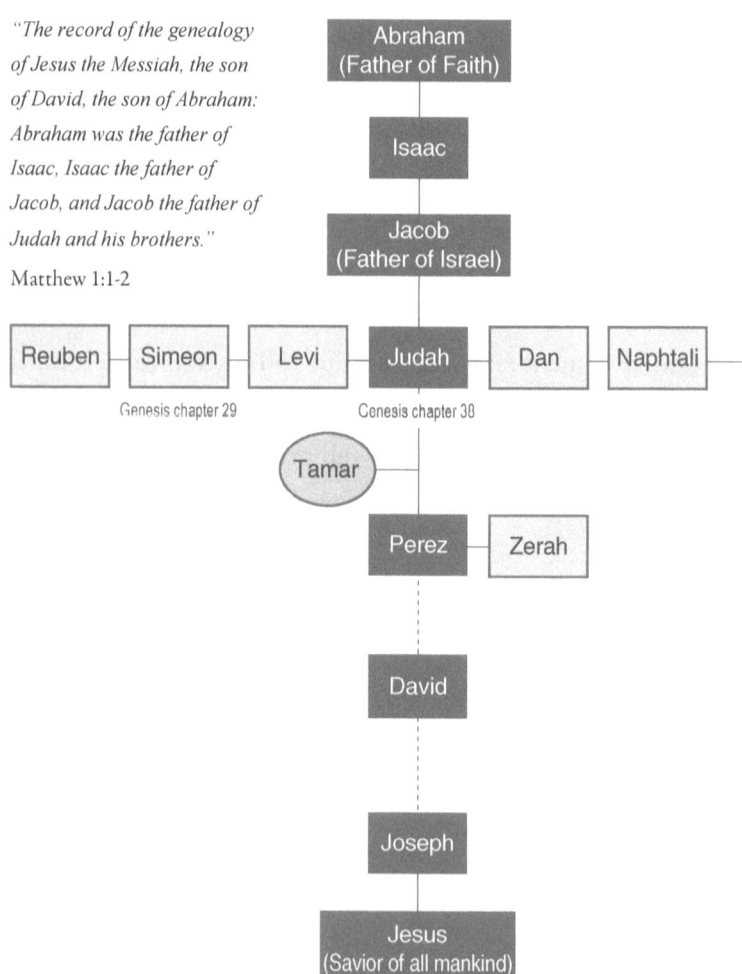

"The record of the genealogy of Jesus the Messiah, the son of David, the son of Abraham: Abraham was the father of Isaac, Isaac the father of Jacob, and Jacob the father of Judah and his brothers."

Matthew 1:1-2

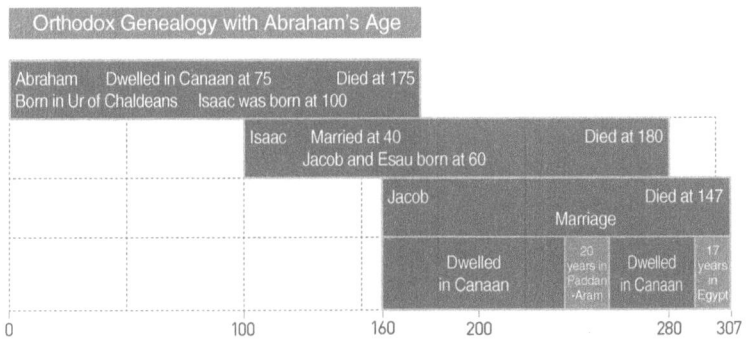

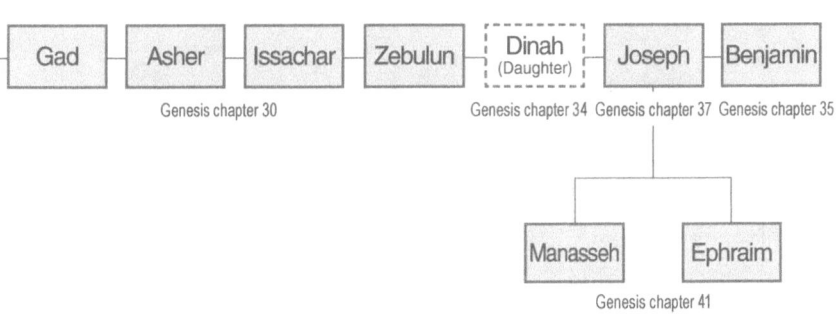

> "So all the generations from Abraham to David are fourteen generations; from David to the deportation to Babylon, fourteen generations; and from the deportation to Babylon to the Messiah, fourteen generations. Now the birth of Jesus Christ was as follows: when His mother Mary had been betrothed to Joseph, before they came together she was found to be with child by the Holy Spirit."
> Matthew 1:17-18

The Old Testament is a Shadow and the New Testament is the Body

1. Difference between 12 Sons of Jacob and 12 Tribes of Israel

12 Sons of Jacob (Genesis 29:32–30:24, 35:18).

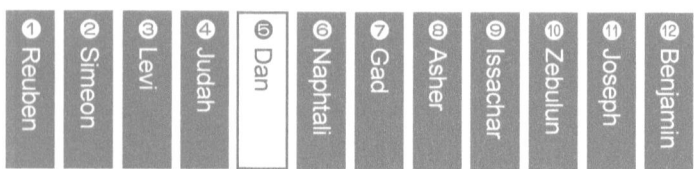

12 Tribes of Israel (Revelation 7:4–8)

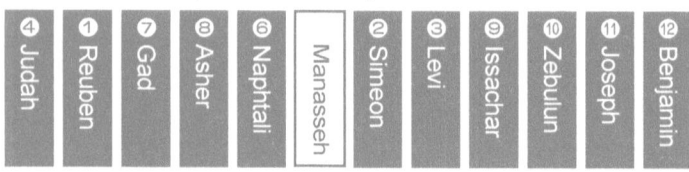

✥ Manasseh replaced Dan that forsook God

2. Difference between 12 Disciples of Jesus and the 12 Apostles of the Lamb

12 Disciples of Jesus (Matthew 10:1–4)

12 Apostles of the Lamb (Acts 1:15–26)

✥ Judas Iscariot betrayed Jesus and was replaced by Mathias

3. The Names Written on the 12 Pearl Gates of New Jerusalem

"...having the glory of God. Her brilliance was like a very costly stone, as a stone of crystal-clear jasper. It had a great and high wall, with twelve gates, and at the gates twelve angels; and names were written on them, which are the names of the twelve tribes of the sons of Israel."
(Revelation 21:11-12)

"And the twelve gates were twelve pearls; each one of the gates was a single pearl. And the street of the city was pure gold, like transparent glass."
(Revelation 21:21)

"There were three gates on the east and three gates on the north and three gates on the south and three gates on the west. And the wall of the city had twelve foundation stones, and on them were the twelve names of the twelve apostles of the Lamb."
(Revelation 21:13-14)

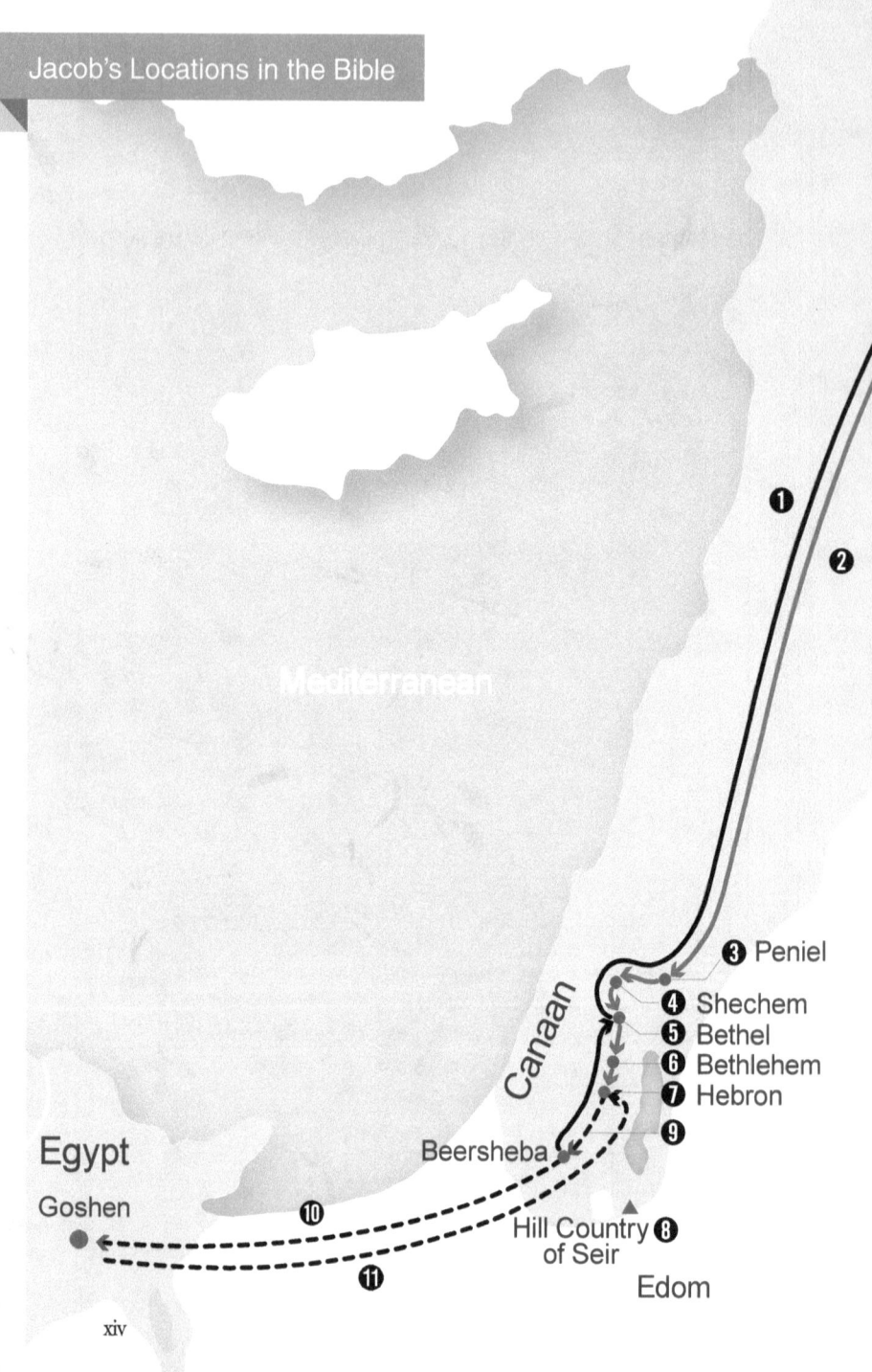

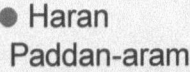

Euphrates River

① Running from his brother, Esau, Jacob goes to Haran (Genesis 28-29)
② Jacob becomes rich and leaves his uncle Laban's house (Genesis 31)
③ Jacob wrestles with an angel at Jabbok River and receives the new name, 'Israel' (Genesis 32)
④ Reconciles with Esau and settles at Shechem in Canaan (Genesis 33)
⑤ Goes to Bethel by the order of God and receives a promise of blessing (Genesis 35:1-15)
⑥ His wife Rachel is buried near Bethlehem (Genesis 35:16-20)
⑦ Goes to Hebron and meets his father Isaac (Genesis 35:27)
⑧ Esau leaves Jacob and dwells at hill country of Seir (Genesis 36)
⑨ Jacob leaves Hebron to move to Egypt and builds an altar at Beersheba (Genesis 46:1-4)
⑩ At age 130, he arrives at Goshen in Egypt where Joseph is the Prime Minister (Genesis 46:28)
⑪ Dies in Egypt at age 147 and was buried in the cave of Machpelah at Hebron in Canaan (Genesis 50)

Table of Contents

Words on Publication
Prologue
    1. Abraham's Orthodox Genealogy and Jacob's 12 sons
    2. The Old Testament is a Shadow
       and the New Testament is the Body
    3. Jacob's Locations in the Bible

Part1
Jacob whom I Have Chosen, I am with You

Chapter 1 The Twin Sons of Isaac · 3

    1. The Older Shall Serve the Younger
    2. Esau Sold His Birthright
    3. The Promise of Blessing Given to Isaac at Gerar
    4. A Hundredfold Blessing Given to Isaac and Three Tests
    5. Peace Treaty with Abimelech at Beersheba
    6. Esau Marries a Gentile Woman

Chapter 2 Isaac Blesses Jacob · 23

    1. Isaac Intends to Bless Esau
    2. Rebekah and Jacob's Cunningness
    3. Jacob Receives Blessings of Firstborn
    4. Esau's Anger and Isaac's Prayer
    5. Esau Wants to Kill Jacob

Chapter 3 The Beginning of Jacob's 20-year Trial · 45

1. Taking a Wife from Uncle Laban's Daughters
2. Esau Tries to Take Back the Birthright
3. God's Promise to Jacob at Bethel
4. Making a Vow before God at Bethel

Chapter 4 Jacob's Unchanging Heart for Rachel · 59

1. Jacob Meets Rachel near Haran
2. Jacob Serves for 7 Years to Get Rachel as His Wife
3. Laban's Deceit and Jacob's Two Wives
4. Leah's Sons - Reuben, Simeon, Levi, and Judah

Chapter 5 Jacob Becomes Very Rich · 77

1. Rachel's Jealousy and another Trial for Jacob
2. Dan and Naphtali Born of Bilhah
3. Gad and Asher Born of Zilpah
4. Issachar, Zebulun, and Dinah Born of Leah
5. Joseph Born of Rachel
6. Agreement between Laban and Jacob
7. Jacob's Cunning Wisdom and 'Law of Looking Forward'

Chapter 6 Preparing for the Return · 101

    1. "Return to the Land of Your Fathers and to Your Relatives"
    2. Jacob Explains Why He Has to Leave Laban
    3. Rachel and Leah's Unvirtuous Answer
    4. Jacob's Family Leaves Laban in Secret
    5. Laban's Chase and God's Protection
    6. Laban's Search for Idols and Jacob's Protest
    7. The Treaty between Laban and Jacob

Chapter 7 Jacob's Victory in Fierce Spiritual Struggle · 125

    1. Seeing the Angels of God
    2. Jacob's Reconciliation Effort with Esau
    3. Jacob's Supplication in the Face of Crisis
    4. Jacob Still Acts at His Discretion
    5. Thigh Socket Dislocated at Jabbok
    6. Your Name Shall Be Israel

Part 2

Descendant of Abraham My Friend,
Surely I will Help You

Chapter 8 Back to Canaan after Twenty Years of Trials · 151

1. Meeting Esau with Boldness and Humbleness
2. Jacob and Esau Reconciled
3. Declining Esau's Kindness to Go to Succoth
4. Reaching Canaan the Land of Promise

Chapter 9 Sin of Simeon and Levi at Shechem · 169

1. Jacob's Daughter Dinah Suffers Shame
2. Hamor and Shechem Suggest Marriage
3. Jacob's Sons Demand Circumcision
4. Jacob's Sons Pay back Evil with Evil

Chapter 10 Preparing the Vessel to Receive God's Blessings · 185

1. Go Up to Bethel and Make an Altar
2. Religious Reformation of Jacob's Family
3. The Whole Family Builds an Altar at Bethel
4. A Nation and a Company of Nations Shall Come from You
5. Symbol of God's Covenant at Bethel
6. Benjamin's Birth and Rachel's Death
7. Leah's First Son Reuben and Concubine Bilhah
8. Jacob Meets His Father Isaac

Chapter 11 Esau's Family Leaves Canaan · 207

    1. Esau's Family Dwells in Seir
    2. Genealogy of Edom's Children and Chiefs
    3. Kings of Edom and Chiefs Thereafter

Chapter 12 Joseph Sold As Slave into Egypt · 219

    1. Joseph Hated by His Brothers
    2. Jacob Keeps Joseph's Dream in Mind
    3. Joseph Goes to Find His Brothers in the Field
    4. Brothers' Attempt on Joseph's Life
    5. Joseph Sold into Egypt
    6. The Sons Lie to Jacob

Chapter 13 Judah and Perez, Orthodox Family of Abraham · 241

    1. Faith of Judah the Fourth Son of Jacob
    2. Curses on Judah's Children
    3. Judah and Tamar His Daughter-In-Law
    4. Judah's Sons Perez and Zerah

Epilogue
    1. Jacob's Confession Reminiscing over His Past
    2. The Twelve Tribes of Israel in Revelation
    3. The Names of the Twelve Tribes on the Twelve Gates
       of New Jerusalem
    4. The Names of the Twelve Apostles
       on the Twelve Foundations of New Jerusalem

"My God,

Throughout my life, I wanted to do everything

The way that I saw fit;

The way I wanted to live,

And in the way I desired for things to be.

I wanted to have what I wanted,

And I wanted to achieve all these things on my own.

But in the end I felt and realized

That it was wrong after all.

Truly, all my thoughts,

All the things that were in my heart,

All my greed and my desire to take things I wanted

Were revealed before God completely

So that I could come forth clean,

So that I could rid myself of all those desires

So that I could I understand

What God's will is and what is true."

- *Part 1* -

Jacob whom I Have Chosen

I am with You

/ Part 1 /

If you insist on your own wisdom and methods, there will be problems in life.

Jacob had an unchanging heart, but he was crafty. He had a strong ego and utilized his own ways and wisdom.

However, through the trials he demolished his own thoughts, methods, and wisdom, and he could see the will of God and he was able to gain the wisdom of goodness.

Jacob

Chapter 1

The Twin Sons of Isaac

The Older Shall Serve the Younger

Esau Sold His Birthright

The Promise of Blessing Given to Isaac at Gerar

A Hundredfold Blessing Given to Isaac and Three Tests

Peace Treaty with Abimelech at Beersheba

Esau Marries a Gentile Woman

1. The Older Shall Serve the Younger

""Now these are the records of the generations of Isaac, Abraham's son: Abraham became the father of Isaac; and Isaac was forty years old when he took Rebekah, the daughter of Bethuel the Aramean of Paddan-aram, the sister of Laban the Aramean, to be his wife. Isaac prayed to the LORD on behalf of his wife, because she was barren; and the LORD answered him and Rebekah his wife conceived. But the children struggled together within her; and she said, 'If it is so, why then am I this way?' So she went to inquire of the LORD. The LORD said to her, 'Two nations are in your womb; and two peoples will be separated from your body; and one people shall be stronger than the other; and the older shall serve the younger.' When her days to be delivered were fulfilled, behold, there were twins in her womb. Now the first came forth red, all over like a hairy garment; and they named him Esau. Afterward his brother came forth with his hand holding on to Esau's heel, so his name was called Jacob; and Isaac

was sixty years old when she gave birth to them" (Genesis 25:19-26).

Jacob's root goes back to Abraham, a man of perfect faith and obedience. Abraham had a son, Isaac whom he begot at the age of 100. Isaac is the seed of promise. He was born solely by the power of God, and even at the moment when he was being sacrificed as a burnt offering, he just believed and followed his father Abraham.

Isaac grew up as a person who served God by the teaching of Abraham. Abraham gave the duty of getting a wife for Isaac to one of his old servants. The old servant went to Abraham's home country and brought Rebekah back as Isaac's bride.

Isaac married Rebekah at the age of 40. But they didn't have a child for 20 years of marriage. Of course, considering the fact that Abraham gave birth to Isaac at the age of 100, it was not very late, but Isaac couldn't wait any longer as he turned 60. He prayed to God earnestly for his wife, Rebekah, to conceive. And God answered him.

Through this event we can see that Isaac had faith and he was guaranteed by God. He learned what faith is from his father, Abraham. He heard and learned about God. He had faith, so he prayed to God about a problem that couldn't be solved by men's strength, and he received the answer.

Yet we can still see the difference between the faith of

Abraham and that of Isaac. Abraham waited 25 years until he got the promised son. It's not that he waited for 25 years when he was young. He had to wait until he became 100. Now, wouldn't it have been better if Abraham had prayed like Isaac and gotten a son earlier?

Abraham did not set a time to receive the answer from his viewpoint. He just entrusted everything into God's hands. On the contrary, Isaac prayed for his desire and received the answer. Of course, this was the fruit of his faith. But Isaac did not entrust everything to God completely like Abraham did. This is the difference between the faith of Abraham and that of Isaac.

Through Isaac's prayer, Rebekah conceived after 20 years of marriage. It was twins. The twins Esau and Jacob struggled against each other even in the womb. Later as the Bible says, Esau had rough character and temper and became a 'man of the field'. Jacob on the other hand was a peaceful man, and he had calm and composed character, but he had cunningness and craftiness.

Esau and Jacob had different personalities and they fought for the head position even in the womb. They were fighting so hard that Rebekah had to ask God what she was supposed to do. God said she had two peoples in her womb, and the older one will serve the younger one.

God meant the older brother Esau will eventually serve his

younger brother Jacob. He prophesied that His providence would be fulfilled through the younger one, Jacob. God's will was determined even before Esau and Jacob were born. But it does not mean God predestines everything and makes everything happen according to His plan.

God chooses people seeing their heart, and He allows them refining trials to lead them according to His plan. Each one will be used as God has planned when they are changed by going through the trials. It was the case with Esau and Jacob, too.

God already saw their hearts when they were in the womb. He saw which one had the upright and proper heart with which they could be used by God. God considers the heart-field, personalities, and characters of each one to allow trials for them and change them.

If God chose Esau and allowed him to go through the 20 years of trials that were given to Jacob, would he have been able to pass them? Esau wouldn't have been able to do that since he had a rough character and short-temperedness. Especially, he did not cherish spiritual things.

On the contrary, Jacob had cunningness and craftiness, but he had spiritual yearning and he had the unchanging heart to accomplish anything if he put his mind to something. That is why he could pass the 20 years of trials, and eventually he became the 'worm Jacob' (Isaiah 41:14). His ego was completely demolished and he came to depend on God alone.

Rebekah gave birth to twin sons. The firstborn was red and hairy, so he was named 'Esau'. The second child held on to Esau's heel, so he was named 'Jacob', which meant 'one who cheats and takes away'. Jacob holding onto Esau's heels means he had the desire to be the head, and it foreshadows what would happen between them.

2. Esau Sold His Birthright

"When the boys grew up, Esau became a skillful hunter, a man of the field, but Jacob was a peaceful man, living in tents. Now Isaac loved Esau, because he had a taste for game, but Rebekah loved Jacob. When Jacob had cooked stew, Esau came in from the field and he was famished; and Esau said to Jacob, 'Please let me have a swallow of that red stuff there, for I am famished.' Therefore his name was called Edom. But Jacob said, 'First sell me your birthright.' Esau said, 'Behold, I am about to die; so of what use then is the birthright to me?' And Jacob said, 'First swear to me'; so he swore to him, and sold his birthright to Jacob. Then Jacob gave Esau bread and lentil stew; and he ate and drank, and rose and went on his way. Thus Esau despised his birthright" (25:27-34).

Esau and Jacob were very different in personality and temperament. Esau was active and he enjoyed hunting in the field. Jacob was calm and he usually stayed in the tent. Isaac loved Esau who was the first son and who took after him. He loved the meat of the animals that Esau hunted, so he loved Esau even more.

We can find a difference between Isaac and Abraham here once again. Abraham loved both Isaac and Ishmael without any favoritism, yet he was not affected by fleshly affection because he knew which son had to carry out God's plan. It was the same when Sarah died and he had six children by a second wife. He only thought about God's will rather than being affected by his emotions. So, except for Isaac, he gave a portion of wealth to each child and sent them away.

But what was the situation with Isaac? From the time the two sons were in the womb, God let Isaac know God's will would be with Jacob and not with Esau (Genesis 25:23). So, if Isaac did not have any favoritism toward Esau due to his fleshly affections, he would have established Jacob as his heir.

But as Isaac continued to favor Esau, the complaints in Jacob's mind grew, as well. Why wouldn't Jacob also want to be loved by his father?

As a result, Jacob resented the fact that his brother was loved more than he was. Also, he resented the fact that Esau had been the firstborn although they were born on the same day. This led Jacob to desire the birthright of the first son. Finally, the desire to take the birthright settled in his heart.

As Jacob was a cunning man, he came up with some ideas to take away the birthright from his brother Esau. He tried to achieve his goal using his brother's short-temperedness and thoughtlessness. But this wisdom was not wisdom of goodness given by God, but fleshly wisdom.

One day, Esau was very hungry when he came back home from the field. Jacob asked him to sell his birthright to him, giving him a bowl of lentil stew. The birthright symbolized the right to receive both physical and materials blessings. They were the right to inherit the father's possessions and the right to continue the orthodox genealogy of their ancestors.

Because he was hungry, Esau made a vow that he would sell his birthright to Jacob. If he thought about the consequences of this act just for a moment, he wouldn't have acted so carelessly. But he sold the birthright because he couldn't deal with his momentary hunger. But Jacob understood the spiritual law very well.

The Bible talks about the importance of the words of lips. Proverbs 13:2 says, *"From the fruit of a man's mouth he enjoys good."* Proverbs 18:21 says, *"Death and life are in the power of the tongue, and those who love it will eat its fruit."* Furthermore, Jacob did pay the price to get the birthright, so the deal was made in spiritual sense.

So, Jacob finally took the birthright from Esau. But by using his own fleshly wisdom and methods it became the beginning of his trials. What if Jacob committed everything to God? Jacob must have heard from his mother what God spoke about him when he was in his mother's womb. If he relied on that word of God, he would have waited until the time of God came. But Jacob couldn't wait.

When we try to accomplish God's will, if we use our own thoughts and methods or wisdom, it might look like things are going well for the moment, but eventually there will certainly be trials. God cannot help but allow the trials to take place because men have to realize how meaningless and useless the wisdom of man is. Having his own crafty wisdom, Jacob couldn't possibly be used by God. For this reason his self and ego had to be demolished somehow.

His craftiness was a form of evil that was in his nature. Therefore, it was difficult for him to realize it and it wasn't something to cast away easily either. That is why a long trial of 20 years was necessary.

Jacob took the birthright from Esau, but the method was not right at all in the sight of God. The birthright is like a symbol of being eligible for God's blessings. Esau had taken it so frivolously that he sold it for a mere bowl of lentil stew. He might have thought he didn't really mean it, but it still shows that he neither cherished nor had longing for spiritual things.

3. Promise of Blessing Given to Isaac at Gerar

"Now there was a famine in the land, besides the previous famine that had occurred in the days of Abraham. So Isaac went to Gerar, to Abimelech king of the Philistines. The LORD appeared to him and said, 'Do not go down to Egypt; stay in the land of which I shall tell you. Sojourn in this land and I will be with you and bless you, for to you and to your descendants I will give all these lands, and I will establish the oath which I swore to your father Abraham. I will multiply your descendants as the stars of heaven, and will give your descendants all these lands; and by your descendants all the nations of the earth shall be blessed; because Abraham obeyed Me and kept My charge, My commandments, My statutes and My laws.' So Isaac lived in Gerar. When the men of the place asked about his wife, he said, 'She is my sister,' for he was afraid to say, 'my wife,' thinking, 'the men of the place might kill me on account of Rebekah, for she is beautiful.' It came about, when he had been there a long time, that Abimelech king of the Philistines looked out through a window, and saw, and behold, Isaac was caressing his wife Rebekah. Then Abimelech called Isaac and said, 'Behold, certainly she is your wife! How then did you say, "She is my sister"?' And Isaac said to him, 'Because I said, "I might

die on account of her.'" Abimelech said, 'What is this you have done to us? One of the people might easily have lain with your wife, and you would have brought guilt upon us.' So Abimelech charged all the people, saying, 'He who touches this man or his wife shall surely be put to death'" (26:1-11).

Isaac left "Beer-lahai-roi" where he had lived for a long time and moved to Gerar of Philistia due to a famine. God once again promised Isaac the Canaan Land and the prosperity of his descendants.

What is the fundamental reason Isaac could receive the promise of this blessing? It's because his father, Abraham, kept God's charge, His statutes and His laws. The grace given to the righteous man Abraham flowed down to his son Isaac, too (Proverbs 20:7). But it doesn't mean Isaac just received all the blessings doing nothing. He also had to show his own faith.

After moving to Gerar, Isaac lied that his wife, Rebekah, was his sister. He was afraid people there would kill him on his wife's account because she was beautiful. But one day Abimelech, the Philistine king, saw Isaac caressing Rebekah.

Abimelech called for Isaac and asked him why he had said Rebekah was his sister. Isaac told him he was afraid, and Abimelech said one of the people might easily have lain with his wife, and he would have brought guilt upon them. Then he warned the people saying if anyone touched her he would be put to death.

God let Abimelech know that Isaac and Rebekah were married, so that nothing shamefully undesirable would take place. Furthermore, God let Isaac be protected by the order of the king.

Through this incident, Isaac realized he had used his fleshly thoughts and had not relied on God completely. Also, he realized deep in his heart that God is the only One who could protect and guide him.

4. A Hundredfold Blessing Given to Isaac and Three Tests

"Now Isaac sowed in that land and reaped in the same year a hundredfold. And the LORD blessed him, and the man became rich, and continued to grow richer until he became very wealthy; for he had possessions of flocks and herds and a great household, so that the Philistines envied him. Now all the wells which his father's servants had dug in the days of Abraham his father, the Philistines stopped up by filling them with earth. Then Abimelech said to Isaac, 'Go away from us, for you are too powerful for us.' And Isaac departed from there and camped in the valley of Gerar, and settled there. Then Isaac dug again the wells of water which had been dug in the days of his father Abraham, for the Philistines had stopped them up after the

death of Abraham; and he gave them the same names which his father had given them. But when Isaac's servants dug in the valley and found there a well of flowing water, the herdsmen of Gerar quarreled with the herdsmen of Isaac, saying, 'The water is ours!' So he named the well Esek, because they contended with him. Then they dug another well, and they quarreled over it too, so he named it Sitnah. He moved away from there and dug another well, and they did not quarrel over it; so he named it Rehoboth, for he said, 'At last the LORD has made room for us, and we will be fruitful in the land.'" (26:12-22).

Isaac farmed in Gerar, and he reaped a hundredfold that year. God blessed him, and his flocks and herds increased and he had many servants. He came there to move away from a famine, and soon he became very rich.

Now, the Philistines became jealous. They didn't like the fact that a foreigner came to their land and became rich. This is the reason they would stop up the wells that Abraham had dug.

Eventually Abimelech asked Isaac to leave the place, for Isaac had become stronger than they. From this we can infer how great the wealth and power was that Isaac possessed. He didn't have only the wealth he inherited from his father Abraham, but he received blessings from God, too. He was prosperous even in a land of the Gentiles.

Concerning the stopping up of the wells, Isaac did not complain or try to reason with them. He had so much power that even the king Abimelech was afraid of him. But he did not have any desire to use his physical power even against those who had harmed him.

Isaac left that place as Abimelech requested and moved to the valley of Gerar. He dug up the wells that Philistines had stopped up after the death of Abraham. When he got water, the herdsmen of Gerar came and argued that it was theirs, although it had been deserted until Isaac dug it again. Isaac did not want to cause any trouble to happen and gave it to them. He named it Esek, which means 'quarrel'.

Isaac dug another well, and again, the herdsmen of Gerar came and quarreled it was theirs. Isaac yielded the well once again and named it Sitnah, which means 'attack and charge'.

We can see Isaac's faith from these incidents. He had learned from his father who said to his nephew, "if [you go] to the left, then I will go to the right; or if to the right, then I will go to the left." Isaac didn't just learn, but he put it into practice in real life. He tried to serve and have peace with everybody even if it meant he had to yield and sacrifice himself.

After Isaac conceded three times and dug another well at another location, there was no more quarrel. Isaac named that well Rehoboth and said, "At last the LORD has made room for us, and we will be fruitful in the land."

It was trials for blessing that Isaac's wells were taken. God wanted to give him a bigger land. What if there were no quarrels over the wells? Isaac would have been content with his situation. Because of the quarrels he kept on moving and this led him to a bigger land. It seemed like he had troubles and he was not protected by God, but at the end of the road we see that it was the way of blessings.

In trials or tests, we should check ourselves as to why those trials came. If they were caused by our fault, we should quickly repent and turn from our previous ways. But if they were given without a cause, we can just follow the way of goodness in thanksgiving. Then, God will certainly pay us back with blessings (1 Peter 2:19-20).

Isaac passed the trials completely with the ways of goodness. As a result, God could give him amazing blessings, and the enemy devil and Satan could not object to it.

5. Peace Treaty with Abimelech at Beersheba

"Then he went up from there to Beersheba. The LORD appeared to him the same night and said, 'I am the God of your father Abraham;

do not fear, for I am with you. I will bless you, and multiply your descendants, for the sake of My servant Abraham.' So he built an altar there and called upon the name of the LORD, and pitched his tent there; and there Isaac's servants dug a well. Then Abimelech came to him from Gerar with his adviser Ahuzzath and Phicol the commander of his army. Isaac said to them, 'Why have you come to me, since you hate me and have sent me away from you?' They said, 'We see plainly that the LORD has been with you; so we said, "Let there now be an oath between us, even between you and us, and let us make a covenant with you, that you will do us no harm, just as we have not touched you and have done to you nothing but good and have sent you away in peace. You are now the blessed of the LORD."' Then he made them a feast, and they ate and drank. In the morning they arose early and exchanged oaths; then Isaac sent them away and they departed from him in peace. Now it came about on the same day, that Isaac's servants came in and told him about the well which they had dug, and said to him, 'We have found water.' So he called it Shibah; therefore the name of the city is Beersheba to this day" (26:23-33).

Isaac went to Beersheba, which is at the southernmost part of Canaan. That night, God appeared to him and gave him a covenant of blessing. He reconfirmed the promise given to Abraham that He would give Canaan Land to his descendants.

After receiving this word of blessing, Isaac built an altar before God and offered a sacrifice just like his father Abraham had done. This was a process to reaffirm the covenant.

He learned the secret of blessings from his father Abraham who built altars and gave burnt offerings everywhere he went. So, God could bless Isaac also, and one of the proofs is that Abimelech the king came to Isaac and asked for a peace treaty.

It's because Abimelech became afraid seeing the evidence that God was with Isaac. Abimelech regretted the fact that he had asked Isaac to depart from his land. He was worried Isaac might have had a desire for vengeance.

Would the king Abimelech come to Isaac if he had wealth and power of an ordinary tribal leader? Of course not! Abimelech's visit to Isaac proves the fact that Isaac's wealth and power were very great now. Also, it means Abimelech acknowledged the fact that God was with Isaac. Although he was a Gentile, Abimelech admitted the fact that there is the LORD God and He is mighty.

This also tells us Isaac spoke about God openly and boldly. Furthermore, because there was the evidence that God was working in Isaac's life, even the king had to submit to him.

Now, how did Isaac treat Abimelech? Although Abimelech drove him away, Isaac did not rebuke him or ask for compensation. He didn't even say any complaining words such as, "How could you do that to me?" But rather, he threw a party for him and treated him nicely until he went back. God is with those who love goodness and follow goodness.

6. Esau Marries a Gentile Woman

> *"When Esau was forty years old he married Judith the daughter of Beeri the Hittite, and Basemath the daughter of Elon the Hittite; and they brought grief to Isaac and Rebekah"* (26:34-35).

We can see why God had to choose Jacob just by seeing the marriage of Esau. Esau took Judith and Basemath, the Hittites, as his wives, whom his parents didn't want. This means he did not care about the fact that his family had to carry on the orthodox bloodline before God. Just by seeing this event we can see what kind of person Esau was.

Well, suppose Esau could have sold his birthright for a bowl of lentil stew because he didn't know better. And yet, if he regarded the birthright important, he should have taken his wives from the people who believed in God. Why wouldn't he know that his grandfather, Abraham, went through all the trouble of sending his old servant to his own country and to his people to get his father Isaac's wife?

Nevertheless, Esau still took Gentile women as his wives. This reckless act of Esau made Isaac and Rebekah grieve. So, we can see the birthright had to actually pass from Esau to Jacob.

Jacob took the birthright from his brother with his cunning wisdom, but he did so because he revered God and longed for spiritual blessings. And about these two persons, the Bible says God loved Jacob and hated Esau (Romans 9:13; Malachi 1:2-3).

'To hate Esau' means God hated his heart that did not care about God's blessings. That is why God had to choose Jacob as the father of Israel His elect right from the beginning.

God is love itself and so He loves all His children, and He wants to give His love in fairness. But because He is a God of justice at the same time, He can give His love only according to justice. After all, our actions will decide whether or not we will be loved by God more, or whether or not our heart will be recognized by God.

Therefore, Esau should have thought about why Jacob was loved by God more, rather than complaining with thoughts like, "Why has my blessing gone to my younger brother Jacob?" Furthermore, he should have tried to take after the good points of his brother. But as we know Esau didn't do it, and eventually his blessing was taken away by Jacob.

Jacob

Chapter 2

Isaac Blesses Jacob

Isaac Intends to Bless Esau

Rebekah and Jacob's Cunningness

Jacob Receives Blessings of Firstborn

Esau's Anger and Isaac's Prayer

Esau Wants to Kill Jacob

1. Isaac Intends to Bless Esau

"Now it came about, when Isaac was old and his eyes were too dim to see, that he called his older son Esau and said to him, 'My son.' And he said to him, 'Here I am.' Isaac said, 'Behold now, I am old and I do not know the day of my death. Now then, please take your gear, your quiver and your bow, and go out to the field and hunt game for me; and prepare a savory dish for me such as I love, and bring it to me that I may eat, so that my soul may bless you before I die'" (27:1-4).

Isaac became old and his eyes were dim. His body became weak. Abraham had perfect faith and he had cast away all forms of evil, and for this reason he was healthy until the day of his death. However, Isaac still had some evil left in him, and he was under the control of natural law.

This difference comes from the difference in faith between Abraham and Isaac. Moses was the most humble and meekest person on the face of the earth and had perfect faith. For this reason his eyes were not dim and he was still strong even at his death (Deuteronomy 34:7). 3 John 1:2 says, *"Beloved, I pray that in all respects you may prosper and be in good health, just as your soul prospers."*

What are the specific reasons why Isaac's body was weak and his eyes were dim in his old age? Isaac discriminated and showed his bias between Esau and Jacob; he sometimes acted at his discretion and did not keep the word of God in his mind; from time to time he did not accept and embrace his family.

He should have looked back on himself and realized his shortcomings, but he just kept on acting as he wished. When his death was near due to old age, he called Esau and wanted to bless only him. He said, "Now then, please take your gear, your quiver and your bow, and go out to the field and hunt game for me; and prepare a savory dish for me such as I love, and bring it to me that I may eat, so that my soul may bless you before I die." The action that Isaac took when he realized he was going to die was very different from that of his father, Abraham.

Abraham gave some possessions to all his children whom he begot through the second wife and then sent them away. Because he loved all his children, he opened a way for all his children and not just for Isaac, to make their livings.

On the contrary, before his death Isaac only thought about Esau whom he favored. That is why he asked Esau to bring a savory dish and he would bless only him. Of course, he could have blessed the firstborn more than the second, but he had no intention to bless both Esau and Jacob. Isaac just did the things as he desired up until the last moment.

From the fact that Isaac asked Esau to bring a savory dish, we can understand the law of the spiritual realm about receiving blessings. As the father, Isaac wanted to bless Esau as much as possible. But blessings do not just come upon anybody just by wishing for them. That is why Isaac made Esau bring the savory dish the way he liked it.

In order to receive God's blessings there must be the process of sowing, which is to show our deeds of faith with our heart. These deeds of faith contain and show the kinds of heart, effort, will, and faith we have.

Elijah asked the widow at Zarephath to serve him with the last bit of food she had, because she had to show a deed of faith before blessing. When the widow sowed with faith, the blessing Elijah had prayed for came upon her household, and the food did not run out until the famine was over.

The same principle applies when we ask to receive something from God through prayer. If we have the faith to receive blessings and answer to prayer, we will definitely show the deeds of faith, which is to show our heart and demonstrate our effort before God. Here, if we have the faith to be able to give to God a savory dish, which is the most precious thing to us, then it can please God.

2. Rebekah and Jacob's Cunningness

"*Rebekah was listening while Isaac spoke to his son Esau. So when Esau went to the field to hunt for game to bring home, Rebekah said to her son Jacob, 'Behold, I heard your father speak to your brother Esau, saying, "Bring me some game and prepare a savory dish for me, that I may eat, and bless you in the presence of the LORD before my death." Now therefore, my son, listen to me as I command you. Go now to the flock and bring me two choice young goats from there, that I may prepare them as a savory dish for your father, such as he loves. Then you shall bring it to your father, that he may eat, so that he may bless you before his death.' Jacob answered his mother Rebekah, 'Behold, Esau my brother is a hairy man and I am a smooth man. Perhaps my father will feel me, then I will be as a deceiver in his sight, and I will bring upon myself a curse and not a blessing.' But his mother said to him, 'Your curse be on me, my son; only obey my voice, and go, get them for me.' So he went and got them, and brought them to his mother; and his mother made savory food such as his father loved*" (27:5-14).

Isaac loved Esau more than he loved Jacob, so he wanted to

bless Esau. But it was not in accordance with God's will.

God had already chosen Jacob over Esau since they were in the womb. Both Isaac and Rebekah knew that fact. And yet, Isaac showed his favoritism until the end. He just wanted to bless Esau only. Rebekah did not have good heartedness either. She also had favoritism. She loved Jacob more than Esau.

When she found out Isaac wanted to bless only Esau, Rebekah wanted Jacob to receive the blessing. She told Jacob about Isaac's plan which she had heard by eavesdropping. And then she gave him a detailed plan. It was a cunning plan to cheat her husband.

She told him to go to the flock and bring two choice young goats from there, and she would prepare them as a savory dish for his father. Then Jacob could bring it to his father and receive the blessing.

Jacob replied, "Behold, Esau my brother is a hairy man and I am a smooth man. Perhaps my father will feel me, then I will be as a deceiver in his sight, and I will bring upon myself a curse and not a blessing."

Jacob knew his father Isaac's words were guaranteed by God. He knew if Isaac blessed or cursed somebody, the blessing or curse would actually come upon that person. Jacob had different physical characteristics than his brother, so he was worried he might be cursed while trying to cheat his father. So, he couldn't accept Rebekah's suggestion right away. He did not refuse it because it was wrong to cheat his father; he refused it only because he was afraid of the consequences if Isaac found out.

If Jacob really followed goodness and the right way, he should have strongly rejected his mother's suggestion. It was to cheat his father, and for his mother it was to cheat her husband. But because he also wanted to receive the blessing so much, he couldn't refuse it.

As Jacob expressed his concern that his father would find out his scheme and he might be cursed and not blessed, Rebekah said let the curse be on her. She spoke so hastily and carelessly because her desire was so strong for Jacob to be blessed.

Proverbs 18:21 says, *"Death and life are in the power of the tongue, and those who love it will eat its fruit."* Rebekah had to suffer throughout her life due to this one thing she had spoken. She had to send away her beloved son Jacob. How heartbroken she must have been for 20 years thinking about her son who was having a hard time in a distant place!

Also, as she knew Esau regarded Jacob as an enemy and wanted to kill him, she couldn't have been at ease even for a moment. As a result of using her fleshly thoughts, the peace in the family was completely shattered. She had to take the painful fruit of her words.

Jacob had the heart that could be used by God, but he still had a lot of things to change, and he also brought trials upon himself due to his greed.

3. Jacob Receives Blessings of Firstborn

"Then Rebekah took the best garments of Esau her elder son, which were with her in the house, and put them on Jacob her younger son. And she put the skins of the young goats on his hands and on the smooth part of his neck. She also gave the savory food and the bread, which she had made, to her son Jacob. Then he came to his father and said, 'My father.' And he said, 'Here I am. Who are you, my son?' Jacob said to his father, 'I am Esau your firstborn; I have done as you told me. Get up, please, sit and eat of my game, that you may bless me.' Isaac said to his son, 'How is it that you have it so quickly, my son?' And he said, 'Because the LORD your God caused it to happen to me.' Then Isaac said to Jacob, 'Please come close, that I may feel you, my son, whether you are really my son Esau or not.' So Jacob came close to Isaac his father, and he felt him and said, 'The voice is the voice of Jacob, but the hands are the hands of Esau.' He did not recognize him, because his hands were hairy like his brother Esau's hands; so he blessed him. And he said, 'Are you really my son Esau?' And he said, 'I am.' So he said, 'Bring it to me, and I will eat of my son's game, that I may bless you.' And he brought it to him, and he

ate; he also brought him wine and he drank. Then his father Isaac said to him, 'Please come close and kiss me, my son.' So he came close and kissed him; and when he smelled the smell of his garments, he blessed him and said, 'See, the smell of my son is like the smell of a field which the LORD has blessed; now may God give you of the dew of heaven, and of the fatness of the earth, and an abundance of grain and new wine; may peoples serve you, and nations bow down to you; be master of your brothers, and may your mother's sons bow down to you. Cursed be those who curse you, and blessed be those who bless you'" (27:15-29).

Rebekah knew very well how precious the blessing for the firstborn was. And she desperately wanted the blessing to go to Jacob, whom she loved. She also had longing for spiritual blessing. We can see from the scene where Rebekah disguised Jacob.

She brought best garments of Esau and put them on Jacob. And to make soft hands and neck of Jacob look like those of Esau, she put the skins of the young goats on his hands and on the smooth part of his neck. There was a reason why she put the best garments before she sent Jacob to receive blessings.

When we ask God for blessings, we have to show the corresponding deeds of faith, and one of the best examples is offerings with all our heart. Another important part is that we have to go before God with a heart that is acceptable to Him.

Garments spiritually represent our heart. The Old Testament was about the actions of keeping the Law, and putting the best garments on symbolizes they prepared acceptable heart before God. Because Rebekah knew the spiritual law about receiving blessings, she let Jacob put on the best garments along with preparing the savory food.

Jacob disguised like Esau and went before Isaac with the savory food and bread that his mother had prepared. He called, "My father". Isaac's eyes were dim and he couldn't clearly see who he was. So he asked, "Here I am. Who are you, my son?" Jacob lied that he was Esau and asked his father to eat the food and bless him.

Isaac was old and both his eyes and body were weak, but he could differentiate the voices of Esau and Jacob. He knew the voice was the voice of Jacob, so he touched his son. But Jacob had hairs just like Esau and there Isaac was deceived.

He said, "The voice is the voice of Jacob, but the hands are the hands of Esau," and decided to bless him. One might think how Isaac could be deceived so easily, but if we really think about Isaac's condition, we can understand this scene.

Isaac wanted to bless only Esau, and he told Esau to bring a savory dish in private. For this reason he could never imagine that Jacob could bring the savory dish. His voice sounded a bit different, but he was relieved after touching his hands. Because he only focused on what he wanted to do, he couldn't thoroughly check the situation completely.

Of course, after all, everything including deception of Isaac was in the providence of God. But if Isaac did not have any selfish motive but only good heart, he wouldn't have been deceived by this cunning scheme of Rebekah and Jacob. Isaac loved only Esau and he wanted to bless only Esau. And because he had this narrow-mindedness and selfish desire, he was deceived in a situation where a true man of God could easily see the truth.

This was the beginning of the trial for the family, and this was not caused by just one person's evil. The four of them showed favoritism, stubborn selfish desire, neglecting the birthright, careless and impulsive behavior, and cunningness. All these mindsets were mixed together and eventually they broke the peace of the family and brought separation, pain, and sorrow upon themselves.

Before he gave the blessing, Isaac wanted to check once again it was Esau who brought the savory food. He said, "Please come close and kiss me, my son." He wanted to check the smell of Esau. Also, kissing represents the spiritual meaning that says, "This son has the birthright to receive the blessing."

Isaac smelled the smell of the garments and became convinced it was Esau. Rebekah had previously deliberated over all these things. She was very meticulous. Isaac was completely deceived by the crafty scheme of Rebekah and Jacob and finally he blessed Jacob.

First, he said, "See, the smell of my son is like the smell of a field which the LORD has blessed." This means the blessing was not given from Isaac at a personal level, but it was given in the name of the LORD God. Next, he said, "now may God give you of the dew of heaven, and of the fatness of the earth, and an abundance of grain and new wine." He gave material blessings in the name of the LORD God here.

But the most important thing is spiritual blessing. In the past, God said to Abraham, "And I will bless those who bless you, and the one who curses you I will curse and in you all the families of the earth will be blessed." This blessing was passed down to Isaac and then to Jacob now.

"May peoples serve you, and nations bow down to you; be master of your brothers, and may your mother's sons bow down to you. Cursed be those who curse you, and blessed be those who bless you." This blessing was given to Jacob personally, but it was also for the nation of Israel, the elect that would come forth through Jacob. That is why Israel will receive the special mercy of God until the last moment of human cultivation.

Why would God allow Jacob to receive the blessing for

the firstborn although he used crafty methods? Though it was cunning, it was different from evil schemes to hurt other people.

For example, Absalom, one of the sons of David, made an elaborate plan to take the throne for himself. He turned the hearts of the people to him through cunning methods. He gathered his power in secret and eventually dethroned David (2 Samuel 15). Such an act of Absalom was caused by an evil heart, and his ending was miserable.

On the contrary, Jacob utilized fleshly thoughts because of his desire, but it wasn't evil desire to do harm to others. Of course, fundamentally it was not right in the sight of God because the method derived from cunningness. So, God just allowed him to receive the blessings but at the same time let him realize his evil deep in the nature and cast it away through trials.

4. Esau's Anger and Isaac's Prayer

"Now it came about, as soon as Isaac had finished blessing Jacob, and Jacob had hardly gone out from the presence of Isaac his father, that Esau came in from his hunting. Then he also made savory food, and brought it to his father; and he said to his father, 'Let my father arise and eat of his son's game, that you may bless me.' Isaac said

to him, 'Who are you?' And he said, 'I am your son, your firstborn, Esau.' Then Isaac trembled violently, and said, 'Who was he then that hunted game and brought it to me, so that I ate of all of it before you came, and blessed him? Yes, and he shall be blessed.' When Esau heard the words of his father, he cried out with an exceedingly great and bitter cry, and said to his father, 'Bless me, even me also, O my father!' And he said, 'Your brother came deceitfully and has taken away your blessing.' Then he said, 'Is he not rightly named Jacob, for he has supplanted me these two times? He took away my birthright, and behold, now he has taken away my blessing.' And he said, 'Have you not reserved a blessing for me?' But Isaac replied to Esau, 'Behold, I have made him your master, and all his relatives I have given to him as servants; and with grain and new wine I have sustained him. Now as for you then, what can I do, my son?' Esau said to his father, 'Do you have only one blessing, my father? Bless me, even me also, O my father.' So Esau lifted his voice and wept. Then Isaac his father answered and said to him, 'Behold, away from the fertility of the earth shall be your dwelling, and away from the dew of heaven from above. By your sword you shall live, and your brother you shall serve; but it shall come about when you become restless, that you will break his yoke from your neck'" (27:30-40).

Soon after Jacob received the blessing for the firstborn and came out, Esau also came back. He made the savory food and went before Isaac. Not knowing what had happened, Esau said,

"Let my father arise and eat of his son's game, that you may bless me."

He was blatantly asking for the blessing, thinking he deserved to receive the blessing for the firstborn. He didn't put on the best garments or have a humble attitude like Jacob did. His attitude was like he had just come to collect what he deserved to receive.

We can see Esau's heart from this, too. He came unprepared into the place to receive the blessing. We can see once again that he had disdain for the birthright.

We can also see how distanced his heart was from goodness. If he had a good heart, when Isaac told him he was going to bless him, he would have thought about the blessing for his brother Jacob as well. But Esau did not even think about Jacob. He just wanted to make the savory food as quickly as possible and receive the blessing.

And when he hunted and made a savory dish, he just asked Isaac to give him all the blessings. We can see how self-centered, selfish, narrow-minded and inconsiderate Esau is.

If he had a broad heart, he would have thought about the standpoint of Jacob his little brother, too. Esau and Jacob were twins but Esau did not care about Jacob at all. He only thought about the blessings that he was to receive. But it turned out that all the blessings were given to Jacob.

Isaac thought he had just blessed Esau, and Esau appeared once again and asked for blessings again. He couldn't help but become bewildered. Soon he realized what was going on and trembled greatly. It wasn't because of embarrassment or anger toward Jacob. It was because he thought he blessed the wrong person in the sight of God.

As explained previously, Isaac called Esau and told him in private, "...and prepare a savory dish for me such as I love, and bring it to me that I may eat, so that my soul may bless you before I die" (Genesis 27:4). Although God had told them that He had chosen Jacob from the womb, Isaac still thought it was God's will to bless the first son, Esau.

Because he had such thoughts, he thought he blessed the wrong person in the sight of God. He didn't know what to do and that is why he 'trembled greatly'.

Isaac knew very well that he could not reverse the blessings that he had given in the name of the LORD God. That is why he said the one who was blessed before him would receive all the blessings. He meant to say he gave all the blessings he could give and it cannot be canceled or reversed.

As he understood the situation, Esau cried and wept saying, "Bless me, even me also, O my father!" He did not even regret selling his birthright for a bowl of lentil stew in the past. He thought he still had the birthright. That is why he thought his father Isaac had to cancel the previous blessing and give it to him. But of course he understood the situation very well, too. That is why he cried and wept.

Esau asked Isaac with weeping, but Isaac could not give him the blessing for the first son that would continue the orthodox family line. He could give only ordinary things. But even in this situation, neither Isaac nor Esau would acknowledge their shortcomings, but only put the blame on the others.

Isaac said, "Your brother came deceitfully and has taken away your blessing." He couldn't realize the wrong he had done, and he was just blaming Jacob. If he thought about why such an event took place in the first place and looked back on himself, God would have given him grace to realize his shortcomings.

But Isaac didn't realize his shortcoming and Esau gave no thought to why such an event took place. He also just put the blame on Jacob mentioning what had happened in the past, too. He did not think about his fault of neglecting the birthright and how wrong it was in the sight of God.

If we likewise put the blame on others, we cannot realize our shortcomings nor can we change. If Esau repented of his wrongdoings at that moment and knelt before God, He would have opened a way of blessing considering his humbleness.

But without realizing how evil his words were, Esau just

kept on asking for blessing as if he were whining. As Esau kept on asking, Isaac said, "Behold, I have made him (Jacob) your master, and all his relatives I have given to him as servants; and with grain and new wine I have sustained him. Now as for you then, what can I do, my son?"

Esau had only one thought that he was the one who was supposed to receive the blessing. And so, he lifted his voice and wept before his father saying, "Do you have only one blessing, my father? Bless me, even me also, O my father."

How heart-broken Isaac must have been seeing his beloved son weeping the way he did? Isaac gave blessing to Esau, but knowing the spiritual law very well, he couldn't give the same blessing that he had given to Jacob. There was nothing he could do but reconfirm the spiritual order that Jacob would be the first and Esau the second.

Isaac said, "Behold, away from the fertility of the earth shall be your dwelling, and away from the dew of heaven from above. By your sword you shall live, and your brother you shall serve; but it shall come about when you become restless, that you will break his yoke from your neck."

'Dwelling' represents where Esau belonged. His dwelling shall be away from the fertility of the earth, and from the dew of heaven from above. It means the blessing of the fertility of the earth and the dew of heaven was given to Jacob, and therefore, Esau would belong under Jacob and receive a portion of Jacob's blessings.

Isaac also said to Esau, "By your sword you shall live." This means Esau could gain as much as he worked hard, and at the same time he would not be protected by God and he would have battles and wars if he departed from God.

Isaac also said, "and your brother you shall serve," and it was to make sure once again the spiritual order between Jacob and Esau. Jacob would be sovereign over Esau; this would belong to that.

It is also said, "but it shall come about when you become restless, that you will break his yoke from your neck." It means the yoke of Esau that bound him under Jacob would be broken only when his life on this earth would be over. But even though the yoke on this earth would be broken, there still is the life after death where they live according to the spiritual order.

In the kingdom of heaven, a very clear order will be established depending on the extent to which we cultivate our heart with the truth and according to our deeds. It is a law of the spiritual realm that we reap what we sow, and we will surely reap according to it.

5. Esau Wants to Kill Jacob

"So Esau bore a grudge against Jacob because of the blessing with which his father had blessed him; and Esau said to himself, 'The days of mourning for my father are near; then I will kill my brother Jacob.' Now when the words of her elder son Esau were reported to Rebekah, she sent and called her younger son Jacob, and said to him, 'Behold your brother Esau is consoling himself concerning you by planning to kill you. Now therefore, my son, obey my voice, and arise, flee to Haran, to my brother Laban! Stay with him a few days, until your brother's fury subsides, until your brother's anger against you subsides and he forgets what you did to him. Then I will send and get you from there. Why should I be bereaved of you both in one day?' Rebekah said to Isaac, 'I am tired of living because of the daughters of Heth; if Jacob takes a wife from the daughters of Heth, like these, from the daughters of the land, what good will my life be to me?'" (27:41-46)

After his blessing was taken away by Jacob, Esau could not forgive him. He held furious resentment and made up his mind to kill him once his father died. We can see he had a very deep root of evil in his heart from this. Perhaps it was possible he hated Jacob, but killing him is something else.

Esau had a very deep root of evil and made up his mind to kill his brother, but he wouldn't carry out his plan until his father would pass away. He thought it was not right for a son to do such an evil act while his father was alive.

Of course, harboring the thought to kill his brother itself is unacceptable to his parents. But in the Old Testament times they were punished for outward actions. So, not carrying out his plan was the least bit of goodness Esau had with which he could be saved later.

After she found out Esau wanted to kill Jacob, Rebekah tried to send Jacob away. The fact that the words of Esau were reported to Rebekah tells us that the anger of Esau was so great.

As things got heated, Rebekah thought her two sons should not be together. But she did not know how deep and great Esau's anger was. She just thought it would cool down if they separated for a while. Rebekah just thought about saving Jacob since Esau was ready to kill him.

So, in order to send Jacob away, she came up with an idea once again. She said to Isaac, "I am tired of living because of the daughters of Heth; if Jacob takes a wife from the daughters of Heth, like these, from the daughters of the land, what good will my life be to me?"

In other words, she meant, "I don't like it that Esau took Gentile wives, and what joy could I have in life if Jacob also takes Gentile wives?" She meant to say they had to send Jacob to the place where their people were to get a wife for him.

With this excuse, Rebekah wanted to send Jacob away to Haran, to her brother Laban's house. Perhaps this looks wise, but the intention in Rebekah's heart was not good at all. She once again deceived her husband and blamed Esau's wives in order to achieve her goal.

Of course, it was not right in the sight of God that Esau had taken Gentile wives. But Rebekah was not speaking for God. She just mentioned Esau's wives to achieve her goal. Her plan might have been a sure way to send away Jacob, but it cannot be said that her intention was good.

Jacob
Chapter 3

The Beginning of Jacob's 20-year Trial

Taking a Wife from Uncle Laban's Daughters
Esau Tries to Take Back the Birthright
God's Promise to Jacob at Bethel
Making a Vow before God at Bethel

1. Taking a Wife from Uncle Laban's Daughters

"So Isaac called Jacob and blessed him and charged him, and said to him, 'You shall not take a wife from the daughters of Canaan. Arise, go to Paddan-aram, to the house of Bethuel your mother's father; and from there take to yourself a wife from the daughters of Laban your mother's brother. May God Almighty bless you and make you fruitful and multiply you, that you may become a company of peoples. May He also give you the blessing of Abraham, to you and to your descendants with you, that you may possess the land of your sojournings, which God gave to Abraham.' Then Isaac sent Jacob away, and he went to Paddan-aram to Laban, son of Bethuel the Aramean, the brother of Rebekah, the mother of Jacob and Esau" (28:1-5).

Rebekah suggested to Isaac they send Jacob to Paddan-aram so he could get a wife there, and it worked. Isaac accepted it, so Jacob could run away from Esau. Isaac called Jacob and blessed him, and advised him to take a wife from the daughters of Laban his mother's brother and not from the daughters of Canaan.

Isaac lacked many things compared to his father Abraham, but he still had enough goodness so he could be used by God in His providence. He knew that he couldn't reverse the blessing that he gave to Jacob, and Jacob alone would receive the full blessing. So, as he was sending Jacob away, he followed the will of God. He once again reminded Jacob of the blessings and sent him away in the blessing of God.

Jacob inherited cunningness from his mother, and he could be used by God only when that cunningness was demolished. For this reason God allowed trials to Jacob, and the beginning of his trials was going to his uncle Laban's house. It was the beginning of his trials, and at the same time it was a necessary step that he had to take.

God let Jacob beget the sons who would form the 12 tribes of Israel later on. Jacob is the beginning of Israel, God's elect. He couldn't take a wife from the Gentiles. So, going to Laban's house served two purposes: allowing trials for Jacob and getting a wife from his own people.

As Isaac advised, Jacob went to Paddan-aram where his uncle Laban was. Paddan-aram was where Abraham and his family once lived (Genesis 11:31). Even after Abraham received a calling of God and moved to Canaan, his brother Nahor and his children were still living there.

Laban was a grandson of Nahor and older brother of Rebekah. Verse 5 says, *"Rebekah, the mother of Jacob and Esau."* Jacob is mentioned before Esau. This is because Rebekah loved Jacob more than Esau and Jacob actually became the heir of Isaac.

2. Esau Tries to Take Back the Birthright

"Now Esau saw that Isaac had blessed Jacob and sent him away to Paddan-aram to take to himself a wife from there, and that when he blessed him he charged him, saying, 'You shall not take a wife from the daughters of Canaan,' and that Jacob had obeyed his father and his mother and had gone to Paddan-aram. So Esau saw that the daughters of Canaan displeased his father Isaac; and Esau went to Ishmael, and married, besides the wives that he had, Mahalath the daughter of Ishmael, Abraham's son, the sister of Nebaioth" (28:6-9).

Jacob left for Paddan-aram immediately. Not understanding the hidden intention of his mother in sending away Jacob, Esau simply thought Jacob was going to their uncle Laban's house to get a wife. So, he felt he needed to get another wife from among his own people, too.

In the past he took the daughters of Heth as he liked, in disobedience to his parents' will. Now he understood that his action displeased not only his mother but also his father Isaac. Up to that point he didn't really care about the fact that his parents were concerned over his wives. But things changed.

The birthright was given to Jacob, and he was going to establish his position more firmly by getting a wife from his own people. Esau thought he would be able to recover his birthright if he killed Jacob. But he realized that there could be problems because of his wives even if he killed Jacob.

The first son has to continue the family line from among his own people, and all Esau's wives were Gentiles, and it caused concerns to his parents. On the contrary, Jacob left for a distant place in obedience to his parents to get a wife from his own people.

Esau felt threatened seeing Jacob's behavior that was very different from his own. He felt he had to get a wife from his own people in order to recover the birthright and take the blessing for himself.

He hurriedly went to Ishmael, the son of his grandfather Abraham and got a wife from his daughters. This act was not out of good intention to follow his parents' will. It was just a formality to have the right appearance as the first son.

We must not just love with words and tongue but in action,

and there must be integrity in it (1 John 3:18). Namely, it has to be truthful action coming out from good heart and intention, but Esau's action was just a means to recover his birthright. So, even though he got a wife from the daughters of Ishmael, it could not please God or his parents.

Esau now had strong emotional attachment to the birthright, and for this reason he had to endure great mental suffering for 20 years until he reconciled with his brother Jacob. He had to suffer from all the hard feelings he had in his heart until Jacob came back home.

Of course, Jacob also was always uncomfortable until he reconciled with Esau. But Esau suffered more, because he held great grudges even to the extent that he wanted to kill Jacob. Therefore, we should understand it is only causing pain upon ourselves if we hold grudges and have hard feelings against somebody. If we harbor such emotions as hatred, envy, and jealousy for a long time, it's not just our mind that suffers, but it would also harm our body.

If Esau forgave Jacob and committed everything to God, he wouldn't have had to suffer for such a long time. If Jacob had also just left everything to God rather than using his own thoughts, he would have suffered from trials and pains for a much shorter period of time.

3. God's Promise to Jacob at Bethel

"Then Jacob departed from Beersheba and went toward Haran. He came to a certain place and spent the night there, because the sun had set; and he took one of the stones of the place and put it under his head, and lay down in that place. He had a dream, and behold, a ladder was set on the earth with its top reaching to heaven; and behold, the angels of God were ascending and descending on it. And behold, the LORD stood above it and said, 'I am the LORD, the God of your father Abraham and the God of Isaac; the land on which you lie, I will give it to you and to your descendants. Your descendants will also be like the dust of the earth, and you will spread out to the west and to the east and to the north and to the south; and in you and in your descendants shall all the families of the earth be blessed. Behold, I am with you and will keep you wherever you go, and will bring you back to this land; for I will not leave you until I have done what I have promised you.' Then Jacob awoke from his sleep and said, 'Surely the LORD is in this place, and I did not know it.' He was afraid and said, 'How awesome is this place! This is none other than the house of God, and this is the gate of heaven.' So Jacob rose early in the morning, and took the stone that he had put under his head and set it up as a pillar and poured oil on its top. He called the name of that place Bethel; however, previously the name of the city had been Luz" (28:10-19).

On his way to Haran, to his uncle Laban's house, Jacob had to spend a night in the field because the sun had set. Lying with his head on a stone and with nobody to turn to, he felt he was completely alone.

Many thoughts came across his mind while he remembered the past. 'I was too eager to receive the blessing.' 'I wish I could still be with my parents.' 'What will happen to me now?' Jacob tried to get to sleep thinking about many things.

And he finally fell asleep, and he saw an amazing scene in his dream. A ladder was set on the earth with its top reaching to heaven. And angels of God were ascending and descending on it. God opened a gate to the third heaven, where there is the kingdom of heaven, in the space of the first heaven where people live. Through this, He let him know that the two spaces are connected to each other.

Acts 7:55 also illustrates a similar scene. It says, *"But being full of the Holy Spirit, he gazed intently into heaven and saw the glory of God, and Jesus standing at the right hand of God."*

Stephen was a sanctified man. Because he didn't have any evil in his heart, he could pray with love even for those who were stoning him saying, *"Lord, do not hold this sin against them!"* At the moment, his spiritual eyes opened and he could see the spiritual realm. How overwhelming it must have been for him when he saw the gate of heaven being opened and the glory of

God and the Lord Jesus standing at the right hand of God.

Jacob also saw the space of the third heaven. The reason why God showed him a ladder was to let him know that the place where Jacob was and the place of God were connected with one another, and the word of God was coming down to him. Of course, it doesn't mean there has to be such as object as a ladder to connect the two spaces. But it's just that God let Jacob feel that there was another kind of space more vividly.

Angels of God delivered the words of God ascending and descending on the ladder. Jacob thought it was a dream, but the same thing was actually taking place in actuality. God told him about the amazing blessing he would receive in the future.

> *"I am the LORD, the God of your father Abraham and the God of Isaac; the land on which you lie, I will give it to you and to your descendants. Your descendants will also be like the dust of the earth, and you will spread out to the west and to the east and to the north and to the south; and in you and in your descendants shall all the families of the earth be blessed. Behold, I am with you and will keep you wherever you go, and will bring you back to this land; for I will not leave you until I have done what I have promised you."*

The events that will be unfolded before Jacob were part of his trials to change him, but in God's broad plan, it was a process to form Israel, His elect. So, God gave him this dream so he could hold on to God's promise and finally overcome.

As he was setting off to a distant place, Jacob was so encouraged by those words of promise that were beyond comparison with anything else. It's because God said he would return home, his descendants would be multiplied, and God would be with him and protect him all the time.

The faithful God kept His promise to Abraham through his son Isaac, and He was going to honor it fully through Jacob now. God always intervenes in delicate ways so that His promises would be fulfilled (Isaiah 55:11).

After Jacob woke up, he said, "Surely the LORD is in this place, and I did not know it." The dream was so vivid that he felt as if God were with him there.

Through this event, Jacob finally understood the providence of God toward him. As he received such a wonderful promise of blessing, he built an altar there to reaffirm the covenant between God and him.

He didn't have anything to offer as a burnt offering for the moment, but he made a vow before God as a symbol that he took God's promise personally. In fact Jacob realized many other things thinking about his situation.

He thought, if he got the birthright, a firm position would be guaranteed for him and only blessings would await, but it seemed things only got worse. He had to leave his home to run away from his brother Esau, and he didn't have anybody to turn to.

And God gave him a promise of amazing blessings. Only then did he realize that everything is in God's providence. At the same time he was awestruck.

That is why he said, *"How awesome is this place! This is none other than the house of God, and this is the gate of heaven."* He said, *"How awesome is this place!"* because he felt the spiritual energy where he met God and heard His voice.

Another reason why Jacob was awestruck was because of his concern that he might have done something against the providence of God by utilizing his fleshly thoughts. He thought that, everything would have been better if he had committed everything into God's hands, but things went wrong as a result of using his fleshly thoughts.

As he met the LORD God and realized His will and providence, he came to repent of his past actions while reflecting upon himself. He put up a pillar with the stone that he had under his head and poured oil on it. Through this, he wanted to reaffirm the covenant between God and himself. Jacob called that place Bethel.

Bethel means the "house of God." Later, after Jacob went

through the 20 years of trials and reconciled with his brother Esau, God called him to Bethel again (Genesis 35:1). God let him officially build an altar there, where He made a covenant of blessing with him. And once again God gave him the new name Israel and gave another word of blessings.

The promise of God was given to Jacob while he was on his way to his uncle Laban, running away from his brother Esau. And this word of God gave him the strength to overcome the forthcoming trials. For the moment, it seemed all things were entangled. But Jacob believed in God who was with him and he was strengthened.

People might use their fleshly thoughts and create a wall of sin before God. But depending on their attitude of heart and further actions in this situation, the outcome may become very different.

Those who love God and are sure of His love can more easily grasp the chances of God's grace. Because they love God, they can more easily feel God's love, too. On the contrary, those who do not love God cannot feel the love of God even though He gives them a chance to receive His grace. Thus, they cannot demolish the wall of sin and fall into despair.

Because Jacob had love for God in his heart, he looked back on himself and repented, and gained new strength when God gave him a chance to do so.

4. Making a Vow before God at Bethel

"Then Jacob made a vow, saying, 'If God will be with me and will keep me on this journey that I take, and will give me food to eat and garments to wear, and I return to my father's house in safety, then the LORD will be my God. This stone, which I have set up as a pillar, will be God's house, and of all that You give me I will surely give a tenth to You'" (28:20-22).

Jacob was running away from his brother Esau. He couldn't be very confident about going to Haran. And what if his uncle wouldn't treat him well? Jacob couldn't help but worry about his unclear future. So, he made a vow that if he could come back to his parents safely, he would only serve God, and the pillar that he had set up would be the house of God, and that he would give God a tenth of his income.

Abraham once gave Melchizedek a tenth of what he had gained. And now, Jacob's vow was establishing a proper concept of tithes. Giving a tenth of all his income means he was acknowledging the fact that God is the ruler of his life and He is the owner of all material things.

Jacob was praying that he would give a tenth to God if God did certain things. And this might look he was giving conditions. But it is not true. He kept in his mind God's word of promise, accepted it with faith, and he verbally spoke of his determination in his prayer to God.

Chapter 4

Jacob's Unchanging Heart for Rachel

Jacob Meets Rachel near Haran

Jacob Serves for 7 Years to Get Rachel as His Wife

Laban's Deceit and Jacob's Two Wives

Leah's Sons - Reuben, Simeon, Levi, and Judah

1. Jacob Meets Rachel near Haran

"Then Jacob went on his journey, and came to the land of the sons of the east. He looked, and saw a well in the field, and behold, three flocks of sheep were lying there beside it, for from that well they watered the flocks. Now the stone on the mouth of the well was large. When all the flocks were gathered there, they would then roll the stone from the mouth of the well and water the sheep, and put the stone back in its place on the mouth of the well. Jacob said to them, 'My brothers, where are you from?' And they said, 'We are from Haran.' He said to them, 'Do you know Laban the son of Nahor?' And they said, 'We know him.' And he said to them, 'Is it well with him?' And they said, 'It is well, and here is Rachel his daughter coming with the sheep.' He said, 'Behold, it is still high day; it is not time for the livestock to be gathered. Water the sheep, and go, pasture them.' But they said, 'We cannot, until all the flocks are gathered, and they roll the stone from the mouth of the well; then we water the sheep.' While he was still *speaking with them, Rachel came with her father's sheep, for she was a shepherdess"* (29:1-9).

Jacob arrived at the land of the sons of the east. "The land of the sons of the east" refers to the area near Haran, at the northwestern part of Mesopotamia. As he reached his destination, Jacob looked around to find his uncle Laban's house. He saw a well. A stone was put on the mouth of this well. Beside the well were three flocks of sheep lying.

Wells for the nomads had very important meaning. They were directly related to their survival, and they would even go to war to secure wells that could water their livestock. So, the shepherds had unwritten rules among themselves.

They wouldn't just water their sheep randomly, but they would open the mouth of the well together after all the flocks have gathered. This way they could avoid any waste of the water as well as any possibility of dispute. And when Jacob arrived there, it was the time for the shepherds to gather to water their sheep.

Jacob politely asked them where they were from in order to confirm his exact location. They were from Haran. Jacob then asked them, "Do you know Laban the son of Nahor?" Nahor is Abraham's younger brother and grandfather of Rebekah, Jacob's mother. And Laban was a grandson of Nahor, and Jacob's uncle.

Fortunately the shepherds knew Laban. They also told Jacob that Laban's daughter Rachel was coming with a flock. Jacob came to Laban without any trouble. So, his mind was at ease, and he advised the shepherds to water the sheep and pasture them a little more because the day was still high.

We can see Jacob's personality here. They were not working for him nor were they his friends. They were totally strangers to him. And yet, he was telling them what to do as if he were giving orders. There was a reason he did so. One of them is because he had diligence and sense of responsibility.

If he were in their shoes, he would have tried to save time as much as possible and pasture the sheep. But the shepherds there didn't do so. They could have let the sheep graze because the day was still high, but they were just waiting for other shepherds at the well. Jacob could not understand their behavior.

In Jacob's eyes they looked irresponsible and lazy. That is why he said in somewhat commanding tone, "Water the sheep, and go, pasture them."

But there was more fundamental reason why he was speaking in a commanding tone. Because he was wise, he learned the mood among the shepherds after exchanging a couple of words with them. When Jacob asked if they knew Laban, they additionally told him his daughter was coming there with the flock. It means Laban was a very well-known figure there.

If Laban had no wealth or power, they couldn't have known him so well. As Jacob figured this point out, he knew that he could exercise influence over those people to some extent, because he was Laban's nephew.

He wanted to brag about the fact that he was Laban's nephew in his mind, and this is the fundamental reason why he spoke in somewhat commanding tone. It is that he wanted to show his power because he thought he had someone powerful behind him. We might try to show off our power and authority by utilizing all the favorable conditions for ourselves. This kind of attitude comes from craftiness.

Those who are crafty know very well what kinds of behaviors will benefit them. If they think a certain side is more beneficial for them, they go to that side. If we know somebody powerful, we might try to exercise their power thinking they have our backs.

But the shepherds there refused Jacob's suggestion immediately. They replied, "We cannot, until all the flocks are gathered, and they roll the stone from the mouth of the well; then we water the sheep."

2. Jacob Serves for 7 Years to Get Rachel as His Wife

"When Jacob saw Rachel the daughter of Laban his mother's brother, and the sheep of Laban his mother's brother, Jacob went up and rolled the stone from the mouth of the well and watered the flock of Laban his mother's brother. Then Jacob kissed Rachel, and lifted his voice and wept. Jacob told Rachel that he was a relative of her father and that he was Rebekah's son, and she ran and told her father. So when Laban heard the news of Jacob his sister's son, he ran to meet him, and embraced him and kissed him and brought him to his house. Then he related to Laban all these things. Laban said to him, 'Surely you are my bone and my flesh.' And he stayed with him a month. Then Laban said to Jacob, 'Because you are my relative, should you therefore serve me for nothing? Tell me, what shall your wages be?' Now Laban had two daughters; the name of the older was Leah, and the name of the younger was Rachel. And Leah's eyes were weak, but Rachel was beautiful of form and face. Now Jacob loved Rachel, so he said, 'I will serve you seven years for your younger daughter Rachel.' Laban said, 'It is better that I give her to you than to give her to another man; stay with me.' So Jacob served seven years for Rachel and they seemed to him but a few days because of his love for her" (29:10-20).

Jacob had already heard from the shepherds about how they managed the well. It was that they could water the sheep only after all the flocks gathered. And yet, when his uncle's daughter Rachel arrived with the flock of his uncle, he immediately rolled the stone from the mouth of the well and watered the flock.

Then he kissed Rachel, and lifted his voice and wept. Jacob told Rachel that he was a nephew of her father Laban being Rebekah's son. He could have revealed his identity as soon as he had seen Rachel but he didn't. He gained the heart of Rachel by doing a favor for her and only then did he reveal his identity.

Of course, Jacob wept because he became emotional. Now he arrived at his uncle's house, and he came to have a sense of comfort. He remembered many things that had happened. But there was another reason why Jacob wept. It was to draw sympathy from Rachel. In that situation, he thought about what kind of behavior would be the best for him, namely, how he could find favor in the other's eyes and get sympathy from her.

As Rachel had this unexpected encounter with his father's nephew Jacob, she ran to her father Laban to tell him about it. When Laban heard the news of Jacob, he ran to meet him and brought him to his house. Then Jacob related to Laban everything. Of course, he wouldn't have told Laban he and his mother Rebekah deceived his father and brother to receive the blessing for the firstborn.

After hearing Jacob's words, Laban said, "Surely you are my

bone and my flesh," and let him stay in his house for a month. Then, Laban said to Jacob, "Because you are my relative, should you therefore serve me for nothing? Tell me, what shall your wages be?" We can infer that Jacob did not just stay there idly but worked for Laban. We can see Jacob's diligence and sense of responsibility.

When he first came to Laban's house, Jacob thought he would go back home after a while. So, if he was a lazy and self-centered person, he would've tried to idle away. But during his stay, he worked as hard as he could to help his uncle Laban with his work.

Laban didn't want to let go of the hard-working Jacob. So he came up with an idea to keep him at his house for a long time. We can imagine Laban's characters to some extent if we consider the fact that he is a brother of Rebekah who had elaborately deceived her husband. Laban used his fleshly wisdom that came out from his cunning characteristics.

Of course, when he asked Jacob, "What shall your wages be?" he really meant it. However, it was so that he could keep Jacob with him by offering Jacob the incentive of his daughters. Here, Jacob made a choice that drove him into trials that lasted a long time.

Laban had two daughters. The first daughter Leah's eyes were weak, but the second daughter Rachel was beautiful. Jacob was in love with the beautiful Rachel. He said he would serve Laban to marry Rachel. Laban immediately accepted his proposal.

From this moment Jacob served Laban for 7 years to get Rachel. But situations changed as he began to work for Laban. Previously he was just helping out with some of the works of his uncle. But now, he became like paid labor who was working with a contract.

Jacob was born and raised in a very prominent family. Thus, being treated as a paid worker itself was a hardship for him. Jacob didn't find it hard to endure 7 years because of his love for Rachel. Of course, this was not true, spiritual love, but we can still feel how great power of love is.

He was working no more as a nephew but as a paid worker, but every time he felt it was hard, he thought of Rachel. 'It's hard now, but I can get my dear Rachel as my wife if I endure just a little more'. This thought gave him the strength to consider the 7 years as several days.

Jacob could endure those years of trials because he had somebody whom he loved and from whom he could take comfort. Jacob had the willpower to achieve a goal he had set. Furthermore, he also had the good character of fulfilling his duties with steadfast, unchanging faithfulness. This is the reason why God used him although he had a cunning character.

God does not look at the outer appearances but He searches the hearts of men. He wants to use the good points of each one. But even though we have good points, we cannot be used by God fully as long as we have untruth in us. For this reason, God allows trials so we can rid ourselves of such untruths.

And when God refines us, He does not just keep on refining us without giving us any rest. He sometimes gives us a moment of rest and also hope. For Jacob, Rachel was the hope and source of strength during his trials. How emotional Jacob must have been when he finally got Rachel as his wife after the 7 years of hard work!

3. Laban's Deceit and Jacob's Two Wives

"Then Jacob said to Laban, 'Give me my wife, for my time is completed, that I may go in to her.' Laban gathered all the men of the place and made a feast. Now in the evening he took his daughter Leah, and brought her to him; and Jacob went in to her. Laban also gave his maid Zilpah to his daughter Leah as a maid. So it came about in the morning that, behold, it was Leah! And he said to Laban, 'What is this you have done to me? Was it not for Rachel that I served with you? Why then have you deceived me?' But Laban said, 'It is not the practice in our place to marry off the younger before the firstborn. Complete the week of this one, and we will give you the other also for

the service which you shall serve with me for another seven years.' Jacob did so and completed her week, and he gave him his daughter Rachel as his wife. Laban also gave his maid Bilhah to his daughter Rachel as her maid. So Jacob went in to Rachel also, and indeed he loved Rachel more than Leah, and he served with Laban for another seven years" (29:21-30).

Jacob did all kinds of dirty and difficult jobs without complaining, for he had the hope that he could get Rachel as his wife. When the 7 years was up, Jacob asked his uncle to give Rachel as his wife. Laban gathered the people and made a feast.

But Laban did not send Rachel but Leah into Jacob's tent for the first night of the wedding. According to the customs at that time the bride covered her face with a veil, and the groom could see her face only the next morning. Jacob slept with Leah not knowing it was her. He realized he was deceived only in the morning.

Jacob protested to Laban saying how he could deceive him after he served Laban for 7 years to get Rachel. Then Laban tried to justify himself saying, "It is not the practice in our place to marry off the younger before the firstborn." If he had no intention to deceive Jacob, he should have explained it to him 7 years ago. So, it means he was just giving excuses for his dishonest action. But it was poor excuse. In fact, his intention was something else.

Laban then offered Jacob another suggestion. He was already married to Leah, and Laban said he would give Jacob Rachel as well on the condition that Jacob should complete the week for Leah and then serve for another 7 years. After all, what Laban wanted was to keep Jacob at his house for an extended period. He knew Jacob wouldn't refuse his proposal about Rachel, and he used this fact to make him serve 7 more years.

Why would Laban go to this extreme to keep Jacob with him? It's because he acquired a great deal of material gain thanks to Jacob. Thanks to the hard work of Jacob, Laban had become a very wealthy man.

Jacob said in Genesis 30:30, *"For you had little before I came and it has increased to a multitude, and the LORD has blessed you wherever I turned."* Laban became much wealthier after Jacob came to him.

Jacob knew he was deceived, but he couldn't help but accept Laban's suggestion because he wanted Rachel. He completed the week and finally got Rachel as his wife, and then served Laban for another 7 years. Even though Laban was not honest, Jacob still kept his end of the bargain to get what he wanted.

This was also a part of the trials for Jacob. Jacob succeeded in deceiving his father Isaac and his brother Esau to receive the blessings of the firstborn. And now, he was also deceived by

Laban just as his father and his brother were deceived. Jacob considered himself wise, but he fell into the crafty trap of his uncle Laban. He reaped what he had sown.

Of course, in the very beginning, it was Jacob who volunteered to serve Laban for 7 years to get Rachel. But what if Laban had been a good-hearted person? He should have given Rachel to Jacob and taken care of them until he went back to his home country. But because Laban was a cunning person, he first thought about what was most beneficial for him.

Through Laban, Jacob had a chance to reflect on himself, especially about his craftiness. It was a chance for him to change. If he had met only those people whom he could easily deceive, he wouldn't have been able to realize his craftiness. While he was serving Laban for another 7 years, he realized that he had once deceived his brother and his father to get the birthright and blessing, and now he was deceived by his uncle.

We might say Jacob gained what he had wanted for the moment, because he got both Leah and Rachel as his wives for his 14 years of service to Laban. But it was the beginning of another wave of trials for Jacob. Laban gave a maid to each of his daughters when they were married to Jacob: Zilpah for Leah and Bilhah for Rachel.

These four women would cause Jacob to feel severely troubled in his heart. It is mainly because Rachel would not be able to give birth to child for some time.

4. Leah's Sons - Reuben, Simeon, Levi, and Judah

> *"Now the LORD saw that Leah was unloved, and He opened her womb, but Rachel was barren. Leah conceived and bore a son and named him Reuben, for she said, 'Because the LORD has seen my affliction; surely now my husband will love me.' Then she conceived again and bore a son and said, 'Because the LORD has heard that I am unloved, He has therefore given me this son also.' So she named him Simeon. She conceived again and bore a son and said, 'Now this time my husband will become attached to me, because I have borne him three sons.' Therefore he was named Levi. And she conceived again and bore a son and said, 'This time I will praise the LORD.' Therefore she named him Judah. Then she stopped bearing"* (29:31-35).

Jacob served his uncle Laban for 14 long years only to get Rachel as his wife. Obviously, he loved Rachel more than Leah. Rachel knew she was loved by Jacob and based on this she looked down on her sister Leah. Furthermore, Rachel did not want to share her husband with Leah at all. She wouldn't accept any interest or love that Jacob had for Leah.

We can easily imagine Leah's frustration. Regardless of her

will, she was given to Jacob by her father. Also, she was higher in the order than Rachel, because she was married first and also she was the older sister. But Rachel was still mistreating Leah only because Jacob loved her more. And yet, Leah couldn't do anything about it, because she also knew Jacob only loved Rachel.

In this situation, God had mercy on Leah who was unloved and opened her womb. By the grace of God, Leah gave birth to four sons: Reuben, Simeon, Levi, and Judah. However, Rachel was barren, and things began to change.

What Leah had been suppressing in her mind until then began to come up. Leah thought she was now loved more than Rachel because she had given birth to four sons while Rachel bore none. This intrigued the jealousy in Leah's heart to be revealed more openly. It's not that Leah had not been jealous, but the situations didn't allow any chance for her jealousy to surface.

Here, we can learn about people's hearts. Until then, Leah had been one-sidedly mistreated by Rachel. She could not enjoy any of the rights of the first wife let alone getting the treatment she deserved as the first daughter. In this situation, God had mercy on her and opened her womb to give her children. Now, if Leah had had good heart, what should she have done?

She should have given thanks for the blessing given now remembering her past. Also, understanding the pains of being mistreated, she should have considered the standpoint of Rachel who was suffering due to her barrenness.

But Leah was very quick in forgetting about her past sufferings. She immediately began to look down on Rachel the moment she realized she had the upper hand in her relationship with her. Both Rachel and Leah wanted to pay back evil with evil due to their jealousy. If she had had a good heart, she would have given thanks thinking about the reason why God opened only her womb and let her bear four sons. But because she realized she was superior now, she tried to monopolize Jacob, just as Rachel had done.

Leah named her first son Reuben, saying, "Because the LORD has seen my affliction; surely now my husband will love me." These words tell us what kinds of sufferings Leah had to go through having to give away her husband to Rachel. It means from that point her husband should love her and she alone should have his love.

Such a desire grew as she gave birth to more sons. After getting the second son, Leah named him Simeon saying, "Because the LORD has heard that I am unloved, He has therefore given me this son also." She was saying God saw that she was not loved by Jacob, and He was on her side.

Leah gave birth to another son and named him Levi saying, "Now this time my husband will become attached to me, because I have borne him three sons." She became confident. She thought she had gotten back her husband whom she had to give up to Rachel.

After she gave birth to the fourth son, she named him Judah saying, "This time I will praise the LORD." She was convinced she had won. Every time she gave birth to a son, she interpreted it in her own way, and rather than giving thanks to God, she wanted to lift herself up.

Jacob
Chapter 5

Jacob Becomes Very Rich

Rachel's Jealousy and another Trial for Jacob

Dan and Naphtali Born of Bilhah

Gad and Asher Born of Zilpah

Issachar, Zebulun, and Dinah Born of Leah

Joseph Born of Rachel

Agreement between Laban and Jacob

Jacob's Cunning Wisdom and 'Law of Looking Forward'

1. Rachel's Jealousy and another Trial for Jacob

"Now when Rachel saw that she bore Jacob no children, she became jealous of her sister; and she said to Jacob, 'Give me children, or else I die.' Then Jacob's anger burned against Rachel, and he said, 'Am I in the place of God, who has withheld from you the fruit of the womb?'" (30:1-2)

Rachel always had a sense of superiority because she had her husband Jacob's love all to herself. But as her sister Leah gave birth to the fourth son, things changed. She became nervous that Jacob might love Leah now. And her feelings of envy and jealousy grew stronger. She even said to Jacob, "Give me children, or else I die."

Even though Rachel couldn't give birth, Jacob's love for her never changed. And yet, Rachel couldn't put up with the situation where it seemed like she was being despised by Leah.

As she had increasingly more thoughts of nervousness, she felt like Jacob's love for her was not the same. Even though she knew it wasn't Jacob's fault that she couldn't conceive, she attacked Jacob with harsh words.

Jacob lost his patience and said angrily, "Am I in the place of God, who has withheld from you the fruit of the womb?" Jacob had great agony until he said this.

Seeing Leah giving birth to 4 sons, Rachel must have tried to conceive, too. So, she didn't like it whenever Jacob went into Leah, and she must have demanded him that he would only go into her. And seeing Leah giving birth to four sons, how upset Rachel must have been!

At first, Jacob felt sorry for Rachel and accepted her complaints, but as it went on for a long time, he eventually exploded. Jacob said the power to let her conceive belongs to God, and it is correct. However, what he intended to say was that it was not his fault but Rachel's. He didn't really mean he relied on God, but he just wanted to avoid the mental pain he had to go through at the moment.

If Jacob sought a way for everybody to have peace relying on God, God would have moved the hearts of each person. If Jacob accepted Rachel and Leah and tried to solve the problem with goodness, even if it meant he would have to endure the sufferings, God would have caused all things to work for good.

But Jacob was not such a person yet. He couldn't accept Rachel and Leah when they were jealous of each other, and their jealousy only grew.

Spiritual love considers standpoints of others and seeks the benefit of others. On the other hand, fleshly love thinks of personal standpoint and personal benefit. Thus, even if they seem to love each other very much in the beginning, their love will cool down and peace will be broken as time passes. They can have peace if they yield to each other and consider the other's standpoint. But they insist on their own ideas and standpoints thereby breaking peace.

It was the case with Jacob, Rachel, and Leah. Jacob invested 14 long years to get Rachel. We can see how much he loved her. But as he reached his limit, he got angry at Rachel. Of course, it was not right for Rachel to be jealous of her sister Leah and to give her husband a hard time. But what if Jacob had tried to comfort Rachel with gentler and better words?

Rachel was nervous thinking her husband might not love her as much as he used to because she was childless. So, if Jacob showed to her that he still loved her, things wouldn't have deteriorated so much. But Jacob finally got angry at Rachel because she was being unreasonable about conception, about which men couldn't do anything.

It's not only Jacob who did not have spiritual love. Neither did Rachel. She acted in rudeness to her husband only because she was jealous of Leah. We cannot find any gentleness in her. She was being so unreasonable saying, "I die." It even looks vicious. If either Jacob or Rachel understood each other's standpoint, things would've been better, but they couldn't.

2. Dan and Naphtali Born of Bilhah

> "She said, 'Here is my maid Bilhah, go in to her that she may bear on my knees, that through her I too may have children.' So she gave him her maid Bilhah as a wife, and Jacob went in to her. Bilhah conceived and bore Jacob a son. Then Rachel said, 'God has vindicated me, and has indeed heard my voice and has given me a son.' Therefore she named him Dan. Rachel's maid Bilhah conceived again and bore Jacob a second son. So Rachel said, 'With mighty wrestlings I have wrestled with my sister, and I have indeed prevailed.' And she named him Naphtali" (30:3-8).

Rachel devised all kinds of methods to win against Leah. She gave her maid Bilhah to her husband to get a son through her.

As Rachel had wished, Bilhah became pregnant and gave birth to a son. Rachel named him Dan saying, "God has vindicated me, and has indeed heard my voice and has given me a son." When Bilhah gave birth to the second son, Rachel named him Naphtali, saying, "With mighty wrestlings I have wrestled with my sister, and I have indeed prevailed."

But even though Rachel got children through her maid, she couldn't be satisfied. It only caused more competition with Leah. Through this, we can see that fleshly thoughts cannot solve the problem; they will only make things worse.

Jacob knew very well how his grandfather Abraham had begotten Isaac. His grandmother Sarah was too old to conceive and so was Abraham. But they gave birth to a son through the power of God.

Therefore, if Jacob truly trusted and relied on God's power, he should have refused Rachel's request. Knowing what kinds of intentions Rachel had when she asked him to go into her maid, he shouldn't have followed her suggestion all the more.

Also, Jacob knows what had happened when Abraham listened to Sarah's words. Of course, back then, Sarah would have done as she wished even if Abraham refused, and that is why Abraham just went along with her suggestion to maintain peace. In the case of Jacob, Rachel could have demanded of him very strongly. So, we might say both Abraham and Jacob followed the suggestions of their wives, but the heart of Abraham and Jacob was very different from each other.

Sarah gave her maid Hagar to Abraham to get a child, and

the maid got pregnant. But Sarah came to suffer because of this. When Hagar knew she was pregnant, she despised her mistress Sarah. Sarah caused this pain upon herself by utilizing her fleshly thoughts. And yet, she put the blame on her husband, Abraham.

What if Jacob were in this situation? Considering his attitude toward Rachel, he would have gotten angry with his wife saying, "You did this to yourself and why are you blaming me now? I haven't done anything wrong, and you must be responsible!"

But Abraham did not speak or act that way. He said, "Behold, your maid is in your power; do to her what is good in your sight" (Genesis 16:6). He didn't get angry with Sarah for her behavior or put the blame on her. He just let Sarah do what she wanted to with her maid. It's not because Abraham did not care about Hagar. He just wanted to commit everything into God's hands and solve the problem in God's ways. As a result, God caused all things to work for good.

The consequences of Sarah implementing her fleshly thoughts were painful. Even after Sarah gave birth to Isaac she had to worry about him because of Ishmael. She reached a situation where she had to come up with another fleshly idea, which was to drive away Ishmael and Hagar once again.

As in Sarah's case, the problem cannot be resolved if fleshly thoughts are used. They will only cause further problems and greater pain. Since Jacob knew about Sarah's case, what should he have done in such a situation?

He should have stopped Rachel because she was following her fleshly thoughts. But he just listened to her. Furthermore, he listened to Leah as well when she gave him her maid to have more children.

Jacob could have thought it was goodness to be fair to both his wives in an attempt to pursue peace. But it was just that, as he accepted a fleshly one, he had to accept another fleshly one again. Even though his intention might have been good, it was only fleshly goodness.

Even though something looks good in men's sight, it can stand against God if it has come from fleshly thoughts. With fleshly thoughts, things might seem to be going well and everybody is happy for the moment, but the final outcome cannot be good. Soon, Jacob realized how foolish it was of him to use fleshly thoughts.

Such process as above to break these fleshly thoughts and deny ourselves is our refining trials. Those things happened due to jealousy between Leah and Rachel, but God allowed such situations so that Jacob could change. God knew what kinds of situations would provoke and reveal deep part of Jacob's heart, and He intervened in delicate ways so that Jacob could realize himself and change.

3. Gad and Asher Born of Zilpah

"When Leah saw that she had stopped bearing, she took her maid Zilpah and gave her to Jacob as a wife. Leah's maid Zilpah bore Jacob a son. Then Leah said, 'How fortunate!' So she named him Gad. Leah's maid Zilpah bore Jacob a second son. Then Leah said, 'Happy am I! For women will call me happy.' So she named him Asher" (30:9-13).

Jealousy between Leah and Rachel drove Jacob's family into greater conflict and dissension. Leah couldn't bear with Rachel when Rachel was happy feeling she triumphed over Leah by giving her maid Bilhah to Jacob and getting two sons.

As she couldn't have any more children, Leah gave her maid Zilpah to Jacob to have more children. So, Jacob had two wives and two concubines, and there was no peace in the family.

Zilpah, who was given to Jacob as a concubine, became pregnant and gave birth to a son as Leah hoped. Leah was happy and named the son 'Gad'. It means 'being fortunate'.

Zilpah became pregnant once again and gave birth to another son. Leah said all women would call her "happy". She named the son 'Asher' which means 'joy'.

4. Issachar, Zebulun, and Dinah Born of Leah

"'Now in the days of wheat harvest Reuben went and found mandrakes in the field, and brought them to his mother Leah. Then Rachel said to Leah, 'Please give me some of your son's mandrakes.' But she said to her, 'Is it a small matter for you to take my husband? And would you take my son's mandrakes also?' So Rachel said, 'Therefore he may lie with you tonight in return for your son's mandrakes.' When Jacob came in from the field in the evening, then Leah went out to meet him and said, 'You must come in to me, for I have surely hired you with my son's mandrakes.' So he lay with her that night. God gave heed to Leah, and she conceived and bore Jacob a fifth son. Then Leah said, 'God has given me my wages because I gave my maid to my husband.' So she named him Issachar. Leah conceived again and bore a sixth son to Jacob. Then Leah said, 'God has endowed me with a good gift; now my husband will dwell with me, because I have borne him six sons.' So she named him Zebulun. Afterward she bore a daughter and named her Dinah" (30:14-21).

Jacob had 4 wives, but his love for Rachel was unwavering. For this reason she almost monopolized the right to claim the husband as a wife.

One day in the days of wheat harvest Reuben went and found mandrakes in the field. Mandrakes were known to be herbs that were good for sexual life and that enabled pregnancy.

Upon hearing Reuben gave mandrakes to Leah, Rachel went to Leah and asked for them. Leah refused saying, "And would you take my son's mandrakes also?"

After all, in order to get the mandrakes, Rachel allowed Leah to lay with the husband. Leah lay with her husband after paying the price of mandrakes and became pregnant. She bore him two more sons and a daughter.

The fifth son was named Issachar. It means 'wages' meaning "God has given me my wages because I gave my maid to my husband." She interpreted the situation as if God gave her a son because He accepted her action of giving her maid to Jacob.

The sixth son's name is Zebulun, meaning 'dwelling'. It means Jacob would dwell with her. It tells us of Leah's desire to take all the love of Jacob. In physical sense, none of Jacob's sons' names has good meaning. Their names were given with the desires to triumph over and to be loved more than the other. Leah and Rachel gave names to their sons thinking with fleshly thoughts that God was on their side respectively.

We can see not only Rachel who couldn't bear any children but also Leah who had already borne many children were very jealous of each other. Envy and jealousy will not stop just because you are ahead in the game or in a position superior to the other. The more you have, the more you desire. Even though you subdued the other completely, your jealousy will come out again if you encounter somebody else.

If you pay back evil with evil, the vicious circle of evil cannot stop. Even if you can completely suppress the other with evil, you will surely receive the retribution for your evil. Even if you don't get it on this earth, you can never avoid the punishment and retribution in the life after death.

5. Joseph Born of Rachel

"Then God remembered Rachel, and God gave heed to her and opened her womb. So she conceived and bore a son and said, 'God has taken away my reproach.' She named him Joseph, saying, 'May the LORD give me another son'" (30:22-24).

Rachel didn't bear any child while Leah bore six sons and a daughter and the two maids bore sons. But finally, Rachel also became pregnant. The Bible says, "God remembered Rachel, and God gave heed to her and opened her womb." It doesn't mean God opened her womb because she was right in the sight of God. God did so in consideration of Jacob.

God knew Jacob's desire. He wanted that a son born of Rachel would continue the orthodox genealogy. That is why God opened Rachel's womb. God remembered that Jacob worked faithfully for 14 years to get Rachel.

When she finally bore the first child that she was longing for so much, Rachel said, "May the LORD give me another son," and named him Joseph. We can feel her desire just by hearing the name. Rather than giving thanks and being content with the grace of God given to her, she wanted to have more in her greed.

Of course, desiring more children of itself is not a fault. It is rather something good to long for God's blessings and make positive remarks with faith. But had Rachel been truly thankful for the grace of God, she wouldn't have named her first son 'Joseph'.

She'd have given a name that meant to praise God such as 'thankfulness', 'glory', 'grace', or 'praise'. But she had strong desire that she wanted to get ahead of Leah by bearing more children.

If we have evil and greed, we'd try to get more rather than give thanks, even if we by the grace of God get something we desired.

When we consider how Rachel and Leah were naming their sons, we can see they are interpreting the situations at their discretion, as they saw fit. They were so preoccupied with seeking their own desires that they couldn't give thanks for God's grace or understand God's will in each matter.

The fundamental reason why they turned out to be the way they were was their jealousy to get Jacob's love all for themselves exclusively. Of course, more fundamentally it was their evil.

However, Jacob also gave rise to his wives' jealousy. He gave special love to Rachel only, knowing very well that they were jealous of each other. This act had impacts on his children, too.

Well, we can understand he loved Rachel, and he couldn't help it. But he shouldn't have let his children feel favoritism. His favoritism caused other children to be jealous of Joseph. In the case of Abraham, even though the orthodoxy would be carried on by Isaac, he did not treat other children lightly. He loved all of them as fairly as possible.

But in the case of Jacob, he gave such special love only to Joseph whom Rachel bore to him. His act caused dissension among the brothers, and eventually this led to the occasion where Joseph was sold as a slave into Egypt at the hand of his brothers.

6. Agreement between Laban and Jacob

"Now it came about when Rachel had borne Joseph, that Jacob said to Laban, 'Send me away, that I may go to my own place and to my own country. Give me my wives and my children for whom I have served you, and let me depart; for you yourself know my service which I have rendered you.' But Laban said to him, 'If now it pleases you, stay with me; I have divined that the LORD has blessed me on your account.' He continued, 'Name me your wages, and I will give it.' But

he said to him, 'You yourself know how I have served you and how your cattle have fared with me. For you had little before I came and it has increased to a multitude, and the LORD has blessed you wherever I turned. But now, when shall I provide for my own household also?' So he said, 'What shall I give you?' And Jacob said, 'You shall not give me anything. If you will do this one thing for me, I will again pasture and keep your flock: let me pass through your entire flock today, removing from there every speckled and spotted sheep and every black one among the lambs and the spotted and speckled among the goats; and such shall be my wages. So my honesty will answer for me later, when you come concerning my wages. Every one that is not speckled and spotted among the goats and black among the lambs, if found with me, will be considered stolen.' Laban said, 'Good, let it be according to your word.' So he removed on that day the striped and spotted male goats and all the speckled and spotted female goats, every one with white in it, and all the black ones among the sheep, and gave them into the care of his sons. And he put a distance of three days' journey between himself and Jacob, and Jacob fed the rest of Laban's flocks" (30:25-36).

After Rachel bore Joseph, Jacob mentioned to Laban his uncle and father-in-law that he wanted to go back to his home land. But he couldn't go back without getting any pay for all his work. That doesn't mean he could just ask Laban to give him his wages. He knew Laban wouldn't just give it away.

So, Jacob led Laban to talk about his wage first. He led his uncle to acknowledge his work by saying, "Give me my wives and my children for whom I have served you, and let me depart; for you yourself know my service which I have rendered you."

Laban acknowledged that he received God's blessings thanks to Jacob. But his answer was not from a genuine heart. He realized Jacob had already made up his mind to go back to his home country, and he wanted to get him to stay even longer. That is why he acknowledged the work of Jacob and made another offer for his wages, so that he might change his mind and stay longer.

As a matter of fact, Laban had already cheated Jacob and changed the wages many times (Genesis 31:7). Yet again, he suggested Jacob stay with him a little longer offering him wages. This time, Laban let Jacob decide his own wage, too.

Jacob was too good a worker to let him just slip away. God blessed the household of Laban because Jacob served and worked for Laban with all his effort and mind. Knowing this fact very well, Laban wanted to stop Jacob from going back to his home country by any means necessary.

One might say Jacob had the upper hand because Laban had to acknowledge his value and he let Jacob also decide his own wage. So, if it were for ordinary people, they'd have just asked for whatever amount of wages they wanted.

But Jacob suggested something that seemed really foolish. He did not ask for any specific amount of wage, but he suggested he would take every speckled and spotted sheep and every black one among the lambs and the spotted and speckled among the goats.

We know well sheep are mostly white. It's not easy for them to be speckled, spotted, or black. Mostly, goats are white or black. Few are spotted and speckled among the goats. If you know livestock just a little bit, you know the situation is very unfavorable for Jacob.

The greedy Laban would never let go of such a chance. He might have thought it was rather strange but clearly it was an offer very favorable to him, and he could never decline such an offer.

Jacob knew very well that Laban wouldn't easily let him have his wages. That is why he had to come up with an idea to get his share. Also, he couldn't let Laban see his secret plan. Jacob made an offer that seemed absolutely favorable for Laban so that Laban would willingly accept it.

Why did Jacob make an offer that seemed very unfavorable to him? He had the confidence that he could get what he wanted and sure faith in God's words given to him.

God said in Genesis 28:15, *"Behold, I am with you and will keep you wherever you go, and will bring you back to this land; for I will not leave you until I have done what I have promised you."* Jacob believed that God would keep him and protect him as God had said.

He also believed in his own wisdom. He was confident that he could get the kinds of sheep and goats using a certain method.

How would Laban have acted in this situation if he had any good heart? Rather than accepting apparently unfavorable offer for Jacob, he should have cared for Jacob and tried to find a better way for him. But Laban immediately took the offer because it looked beneficial for him. If we think about his later actions, we can see very well he only tried to serve his own interests.

On that day, Laban separated the flock and gave Jacob only white sheep and goats, and black goats. He gave the rest to his sons and put a distance of three days' journey between himself and Jacob. It was so that his sheep or goats wouldn't get mixed up with Jacob's, and there wouldn't be any spotted or speckled animals.

How stingy he was! He tried all his best to stop spotted or speckled animals from being born.

7. Jacob's Cunning Wisdom and 'Law of Looking Forward'

"Then Jacob took fresh rods of poplar and almond and plane trees, and peeled white stripes in them, exposing the white which was in the rods. He set the rods which he had peeled in front of the flocks in the gutters, even in the watering troughs, where the flocks came to drink; and they mated when they came to drink. So the flocks mated by the rods, and the flocks brought forth striped, speckled, and spotted. Jacob separated the lambs, and made the flocks face toward the striped and all the black in the flock of Laban; and he put his own herds apart, and did not put them with Laban's flock. Moreover, whenever the stronger of the flock were mating, Jacob would place the rods in the sight of the flock in the gutters, so that they might mate by the rods; but when the flock was feeble, he did not put them in; so the feebler were Laban's and the stronger Jacob's. So the man became exceedingly prosperous, and had large flocks and female and male servants and camels and donkeys" (30:37-43).

Laban did everything in his power to ensure his benefit, but God was on Jacob's side. Jacob soon became very wealthy by God's help given upon Jacob's wisdom. Jacob's wisdom is the 'law of looking forward with faith', or the 'law of looking forward' in short.

The bark of poplar and almond and plane trees are blackish or dark brown. On the other hand, the inside is white and glossy. So, if you peel the bark off here and there, it will have black and white pattern. Jacob put these rods where the stronger of the flock were mating, so that they would look at those rods while they were mating. And as a matter of fact, the lambs that were born were actually striped, speckled, and spotted.

The law of looking forward with faith is not just to look forward to something but also to harbor it in heart. This law can be applied in many aspects. For example, one's life can become different depending on which person they look up to in their childhood.

Especially our faith can become very different according to which people we respect and try to resemble. The faith of the children is affected the most by their parents. And grown up adults are affected by others, too.

So, who should we look up in our faith? It's Jesus Christ, the author and perfecter of faith (Hebrews 12:2). We should be changed beautifully taking after the heart and holy deeds of the Lord.

Jacob began to store up so much wealth by applying the 'law of looking forward'. But Jacob did not apply this method just to get the pay he deserved to get. His method was that he would make the flock see the rods that had black and white patterns so their lambs would be striped, speckled, or spotted, too.

And furthermore, Jacob separated the lambs, and made the flocks of Laban face toward the striped and all the black in the flock of Jacob. This means he made the flock of Laban see the striped and black flock all the time.

On top of making the flock see the patterned rods while mating, he made the white flock of Laban see the striped and black sheep all the time. In this way, Laban's flock would also give birth to striped, speckled, or spotted lambs more.

It also says, "[Jacob] put his own herds apart, and did not put them with Laban's flock." What is the reason behind this? Jacob wanted to make the stronger ones his and the weaker ones Laban's.

Jacob's desire to get his pay from Laban, who had cheated him many times, can be understood. But it was not just that. He devised a cunning method to make Laban's strong flock his.

Jacob relied on God, but he was still using his own thoughts. For this reason, God still had to refine him, so he could change.

To rely on God means complete trust. Jacob thought he trusted and relied on God, but he always used his own methods. He used his own wisdom when he got the birthright from Esau; when he received the blessing from his father Isaac; and when he was trying to get the pay he deserved.

Perhaps he could have thought, "God has destined that

I have the birthright, and it is only natural that I receive the blessing from my father, Isaac." or "I am only taking what I deserve to receive for my hard work." But in fact he shouldn't have put himself ahead all the more for those reasons. This means, if he really believed he'd have the birthright and the blessing for the firstborn by the providence of God, and if he was really taking only the pay he deserved to get, then, he should have let God handle everything.

The work of God will be completely different depending on whether we rely on Him and commit everything to Him or we use our own thoughts. In any matter, if we commit everything to God and pray, He will take the responsibility. But surprisingly many people use their own methods even though they say they obey the word of God.

It was the case with Jacob, too. The 'law of looking forward' by itself was wisdom given by God. But Jacob did not apply the method in a way that was completely coherent with God's will. Of course, he could have said, "I couldn't help but do it this way because there was no way I could receive the just pay from Laban." But we know God blessed Abraham, even though Abraham was in much more difficult situations than those of Jacob.

In Genesis chapter 20, Abraham's wife, Sarah, was taken by Abimelech the king of Gerar. So, God worked in Abimelech's dream to return Sarah to Abraham. Abimelech did not just return Sarah, but he also gave the flock, cattle, and even servants to Abraham.

It was a situation that was just impossible to solve with human methods. But by the work of God, this incident turned into blessing. As in this case, what kind of situation we are facing is not the important thing. With God's work, there is nothing impossible, and we can receive blessings and answers to problems in any situation or condition.

Jacob

Chapter 6

Preparing for the Return

"Return to the Land of Your Fathers and to Your Relatives"

Jacob Explains Why He Has to Leave Laban

Rachel and Leah's Unvirtuous Answer

Jacob's Family Leaves Laban in Secret

Laban's Chase and God's Protection

Laban's Search for Idols and Jacob's Protest

The Treaty between Laban and Jacob

1. "Return to the Land of Your Fathers and to Your Relatives"

"Now Jacob heard the words of Laban's sons, saying, 'Jacob has taken away all that was our father's, and from what belonged to our father he has made all this wealth.' Jacob saw the attitude of Laban, and behold, it was not friendly toward him as it had been in the past. Then the LORD said to Jacob, 'Return to the land of your fathers and to your relatives, and I will be with you'" (31:1-3).

Jacob lived in his uncle's house, but it was also his father-in-law's house. He was also like a paid worker in the household. He always had to watch how the wind was blowing among the people. As his flock increased, he also had to watch Laban's situations. Sure enough, as Jacob's possessions increased, Laban and his sons began to reveal their uncomfortable feelings.

One day, Laban's sons said, "Jacob has taken away all that was our father's, and from what belonged to our father he has made all this wealth." Laban's attitude toward Jacob was not as friendly as it had been in the past.

Through this, we can see what the fleshly man's heart is like. Man of flesh cannot rejoice when others are well off. But rather they are busy keeping others in check in order to avoid any disadvantage or harm to themselves. As the wealth increased, Jacob tried to keep Laban in check, as Laban did regarding Jacob.

Each sought only their own benefits, and it was only natural that the peace would break between them. We can have peace with everyone only when we cast away all envy and jealousy and cultivate spiritual love with which we can rejoice with the truth.

Also as for men of flesh, though not intentionally, they might say something that can alienate people from each other. Jacob's increase in wealth also meant increase in Laban's wealth. So, if Laban's sons had spoken to Laban only good things about Jacob, the peace wouldn't have been broken.

Proverbs 17:9 says, *"He who conceals a transgression seeks love, but he who repeats a matter separates intimate friends."* If Laban's sons had more goodness, they could have acknowledged Jacob's wealth as God's blessings thinking, "God is giving to Jacob for the hard-work he has rendered until now."

But they just thought Jacob was stealing from their father's possessions and the thoughts were expressed openly in front of Laban. The relationship between Laban and Jacob only deteriorated because of these malevolent sons of Laban.

Finally, the situation forced Jacob to leave Laban. Knowing this situation, God told Jacob, "Return to the land of your fathers and to your relatives, and I will be with you." God let him know that it was time for him to return to his home land.

2. Jacob Explains Why He Has to Leave Laban

"So Jacob sent and called Rachel and Leah to his flock in the field, and said to them, 'I see your father's attitude, that it is not friendly toward me as formerly, but the God of my father has been with me. You know that I have served your father with all my strength. Yet your father has cheated me and changed my wages ten times; however, God did not allow him to hurt me. If he spoke thus, "The speckled shall be your wages," then all the flock brought forth speckled; and if he spoke thus, "The striped shall be your wages," then all the flock brought forth striped. Thus God has taken away your father's livestock and given them to me. And it came about at the time when the flock were mating that I lifted up my eyes and saw in a dream, and behold, the male goats which were mating were striped, speckled, and mottled. Then the angel of God said to me in the dream, "Jacob," and I said, "Here I am." He said, "Lift up now your eyes and see that all the male goats which are mating are striped, speckled, and mottled;

for I have seen all that Laban has been doing to you. I am the God of Bethel, where you anointed a pillar, where you made a vow to Me; now arise, leave this land, and return to the land of your birth"'" (31:4-13).

One night an angel of God appeared in Jacob's dream and instructed him to go back to the land of his birth, reminding him of the promise he had made in Bethel 20 years ago. Jacob in obedience began to prepare to return to his homeland.

First he called Rachel and Leah and explained to them their father Laban's attitude toward him was different now. He also added Laban had changed his wage ten times to explain that he had been mistreated. But he didn't have to mention this. He could have just said it was time for him to return to his homeland in the providence of God. But he repeatedly said he was mistreated even though he served Laban with all his best.

He put all the blame on Laban and interpreted everything in his favor. He even mentioned the name of God to justify himself. Namely, he said God took the flock from Laban and gave it to him because he was right and he deserved it. Jacob increased his wealth based on the possessions of Laban, and yet, he just says everything was in the providence of God.

He also told his wives about the dream God had given to him. It was a dream that he had had during the mating season of the flock after he made an agreement on his wages with Laban. In his dream he saw all the male goats which were mating were striped, speckled, and mottled.

He also said, in his dream an angel of the LORD said to him, "Lift up now your eyes and see that all the male goats which are mating are striped, speckled, and mottled; for I have seen all that Laban has been doing to you." If you just hear his story, it sounds like it was completely by God's work that he gained the flock that were striped, speckled, and mottled. But in fact, it was all Jacob's idea. Nevertheless, God allowed him to have such a dream and accumulate wealth because He wanted to let him reap the fruit of his faithful work until then.

God was with Jacob and protected him to receive blessings, but it's not that God made Jacob use the method he used. Jacob gained wealth by putting in effect the 'law of looking forward', which was wisdom given by God. And yet, Jacob was speaking as though God attested to everything he had done.

If Jacob had been really good-hearted here, he wouldn't have revealed the unfair treatment of Laban in order to justify himself. Also, he wouldn't have tried to make it look like it was God's will when he was only acting according to his own thoughts and wisdom.

Men of flesh reveal the fault of others when they need to justify themselves. It's because they think others will consider them right when they capitalize the faults of others.

Or, they try to put the blame on others in order to justify themselves. They say such things as, "How can you hold me responsible while all others are doing the same thing?"

In some cases, they try to justify their behaviors by saying they did what they had done according to the will and providence of God. If anything goes wrong, they put the blame on others, and if anything turns out well for them, they say it is God's will and they try to continue.

Jacob had been in refining trials for a long time while he was with Laban. Yet he was still using his own thoughts and methods. It was in the providence of God that he should return to the land of his birth, but what he had done was not right.

He should have tried to melt Laban's heart or thought of ways to have peace with him. But he was only busy trying to avoid uncomfortable situations while keeping all his things as well. The biggest reason why Jacob wanted to leave quickly was that he wanted to avoid conflicts with Laban or his sons.

If he had the heart like that of his grandfather Abraham, who was able to say, "If to the left, then I will go to the right; or if to the right, then I will go to the left" then, he wouldn't have tried to leave as if he were running away. He'd have wrapped up everything and every relationship properly before he left. Of course, to have peace with Laban, Jacob could have had to give some of his possessions to Laban, too.

But he was not willing to do so just to have peace with Laban. He had greater desire to keep his possessions than to pursue peace. So, as soon as his wives agreed, he left with all his children and possessions, without saying anything to Laban.

3. Rachel and Leah's Unvirtuous Answer

"Rachel and Leah said to him, 'Do we still have any portion or inheritance in our father's house? Are we not reckoned by him as foreigners? For he has sold us, and has also entirely consumed our purchase price. Surely all the wealth which God has taken away from our father belongs to us and our children; now then, do whatever God has said to you'" (31:14-16).

Rachel and Leah readily accepted the suggestion of their husband Jacob to go back to his homeland. But, they also had their ulterior motives. It's that they had many complaints against their father, mostly because of the matter of possessions.

Their greed for wealth was revealed in their words saying, "Surely all the wealth which God has taken away from our father belongs to us and our children." It tells us that they agreed to Jacob's suggestion not only because of the mistreatment of Laban.

Outwardly they said to Jacob, "do whatever God has said to

you." But in their mind, they wanted to seek their own benefit and keep their wealth.

They thought they and their children had more future by being sided with Jacob rather than their father Laban. For this reason, they even abandoned their duty to their father.

If Rachel and Leah would fulfill their duty to their father, what would they have done when they heard Jacob's suggestion? First, they'd have tried to find a way to pacify their father and their husband. But because they were also self-seeking, they completely agreed with their husband only.

As things were seemingly going smoothly, Jacob must have thought it was the right time for him to return to the land of his birth by the blessing of God in His providence. He'd have thought he was following the will of God very well, too. But in fact, the untruth he had was delicately mixed with the truth and he mistakenly thought his acts were of truth. Jacob had self-seeking desire to follow his own thoughts and methods, but he did not realize it. For this reason God let him break his 'self' completely at the Jabbok River.

4. Jacob's Family Leaves Laban in Secret

"Then Jacob arose and put his children and his wives upon

camels; and he drove away all his livestock and all his property which he had gathered, his acquired livestock which he had gathered in Paddan-aram, to go to the land of Canaan to his father Isaac. When Laban had gone to shear his flock, then Rachel stole the household idols that were her father's. And Jacob deceived Laban the Aramean by not telling him that he was fleeing. So he fled with all that he had; and he arose and crossed the Euphrates River, and set his face toward the hill country of Gilead. When it was told Laban on the third day that Jacob had fled," (31:17-22)

Finally, Jacob set out for Canaan with all his livestock and possessions that he had gained in Paddan-aram. It was a shearing season and Laban was out for shearing. Jacob took this window of opportunity to flee. He knew Laban wouldn't simply let him go.

Jacob had many camels and donkeys and his flock was large. He had already become a very wealthy man. So, it was not easy to take all the livestock and possessions and leave. So, seeing how he acted, we can see he had been preparing for that day anticipating such a day would come.

Jacob also chose the time when Laban was away for shearing of the sheep. He had been preparing to take all his possessions without letting Laban make note of it. He chose the best moment while watching Laban's situation all the time.

But there was one thing that happened unexpectedly. Rachel

stole the household idols from her father Laban. They were used mostly for fortune-telling. Laban was the grandson of Nahor, who was Abraham's brother, and thus a relative of Jacob. But the Bible refers to him as an 'Aramean'. It tells us he did not serve God while living among the Gentiles. That is why he had the household idols that were used for fortune-telling by the people.

The reason why Rachel stole the idols was not because they were expensive. It was a payback for the hard feelings that she had toward her father. She wanted to damage her father mentally by stealing the idols on which he had emotional reliance.

Such an act was caused by the evil mind she had to pay back the suffering she had sustained. It is the case in which a person causes harm to another through what the other party cherishes or they reveal the weakest point of others to cause emotional damage to them.

Jacob set out toward the hill country of Gilead with all his family and possessions, unaware of the fact that Rachel stole the household idols.

5. Laban's Chase and God's Protection

"...then he took his kinsmen with him and pursued him a distance

of seven days' journey, and he overtook him in the hill country of Gilead. God came to Laban the Aramean in a dream of the night and said to him, 'Be careful that you do not speak to Jacob either good or bad.' Laban caught up with Jacob. Now Jacob had pitched his tent in the hill country, and Laban with his kinsmen camped in the hill country of Gilead. Then Laban said to Jacob, 'What have you done by deceiving me and carrying away my daughters like captives of the sword? Why did you flee secretly and deceive me, and did not tell me so that I might have sent you away with joy and with songs, with timbrel and with lyre; and did not allow me to kiss my sons and my daughters? Now you have done foolishly. It is in my power to do you harm, but the God of your father spoke to me last night, saying, "Be careful not to speak either good or bad to Jacob." Now you have indeed gone away because you longed greatly for your father's house; but why did you steal my gods?' Then Jacob replied to Laban, 'Because I was afraid, for I thought that you would take your daughters from me by force. The one with whom you find your gods shall not live; in the presence of our kinsmen point out what is yours among my belongings and take it for yourself.' For Jacob did not know that Rachel had stolen them" (31:23-32).

Laban heard the news of Jacob's fleeing after 3 days. He gathered his kinsmen and pursued him. Laban was very angry that Jacob ran away. He took Jacob in, provided him with food and a roof over his head. He even gave him his two daughters as wives so he could have a family. On top of that he made him rich, too. He was angry that Jacob left without saying anything. But this is only the viewpoint of Laban.

Jacob's standpoint was very different. He could say things like, "If I told Laban, he wouldn't have let me go easily. I worked more than what Laban had provided me with." Those who seek their own benefit first think about their own standpoints.

Laban was upset thinking that Jacob did not remember the things he had received from Laban. But it's because Laban did not think about Jacob's hard work at all. He didn't think about the fact that he mistreated Jacob in such a way that Jacob had to be very careful about leaving him. And yet, he was just angry only with the fact that Jacob left without saying a word.

If Laban had any goodness, he would have tried to understand Jacob, thinking about why Jacob had to leave in secret. But Laban couldn't even consider such things.

Those who have goodness in heart will consider other people's standpoints, circumstances, and the levels of faith, even when they do something that can't be understood at all. Those who are good do not remember faults of others but only good points. They don't have any hard feelings even if others forget the grace they received.

But because Laban was self-seeking, Jacob's action upset him very much. Especially, when he found out that his household idols were missing, he couldn't control his temper and began his pursuit with his kinsmen right away. Because he was very angry, Laban wouldn't just leave Jacob's family alone.

But just before Laban caught up with Jacob's family, God appeared to Laban in his dream and said, "Be careful that you do not speak to Jacob either good or bad." Laban didn't serve God but at least he knew about God.

In Genesis 30:27, Laban said to Jacob, *"If now it pleases you, stay with me; I have divined that the LORD has blessed me on your account."* He also said in Genesis 31:29, *"It is in my power to do you harm, but the God of your father spoke to me last night, saying, 'Be careful not to speak either good or bad to Jacob.'"*

Laban knew the mightiness of God. For this reason, even though he was very angry at Jacob, he didn't dare stand against God. He had a burning temper inside, but he couldn't say anything.

Laban caught up with Jacob in the hill country of Gilead. He rebukes Jacob, saying Jacob threatened his two daughters and ran away. He says he was ready to send Jacob and his family off nicely with a farewell party, and it was Jacob who prevented him from saying goodbye to his daughters and grandchildren.

If what Laban said was true, he wouldn't have pursued Jacob in such a hurry, as if he was chasing a thief. If Laban's intentions were pure, God wouldn't have to appear in his dream to stop him from harming Jacob. Surely Laban had the intention to harm Jacob when he began his pursuit. Knowing this very well, God appeared in his dream to protect Jacob.

Laban, however, tried to justify his chase, without mentioning his intentions. So, now, he brags about his power with which he could harm Jacob. He says he wouldn't nevertheless harm Jacob because God told him in his dream not to speak either good or bad to Jacob. It means he was holding his anger because of God, even though he could harm Jacob immediately.

In the end Laban allowed Jacob to return to the land of his birth because of his fear of God. But he didn't want to let Jacob go easily, and now he tries to make trouble with the missing household idols. He wouldn't stop Jacob from going back to his home country, but he wouldn't tolerate the stealing of the household idols.

Jacob explained why he decided to leave secretly and that he was innocent. First, he said he left without telling Laban because he was afraid Laban would take away Rachel and Leah from him. But it was not true. He left because he wanted to keep his possessions. It was just an excuse.

Certainly it was wrong of Jacob that he did not show proper respect to his uncle by secretly leaving him, but he was just trying to dodge the reproach by giving an excuse. Being unware of the fact that Rachel had stolen the household idols, he confidently told Laban to search for them among the people of Jacob. Furthermore, he pronounced, "The one with whom you find your gods shall not live."

6. Laban's Search for Idols and Jacob's Protest

"So Laban went into Jacob's tent and into Leah's tent and into the tent of the two maids, but he did not find them. Then he went out of Leah's tent and entered Rachel's tent. Now Rachel had taken the household idols and put them in the camel's saddle, and she sat on them. And Laban felt through all the tent but did not find them. She said to her father, 'Let not my lord be angry that I cannot rise before you, for the manner of women is upon me.' So he searched but did not find the household idols. Then Jacob became angry and contended with Laban; and Jacob said to Laban, 'What is my transgression? What is my sin that you have hotly pursued me? Though you have felt through all my goods, what have you found of all your household goods? Set it here before my kinsmen and your kinsmen, that they may decide between us two. These twenty years I have been with you; your ewes and your female goats have not miscarried, nor have I eaten the rams of your flocks. That which was torn of beasts I did not bring to you; I bore the loss of it myself. You required it of my hand whether stolen by day or stolen by night. Thus I was: by day the heat consumed me and the frost by night, and my sleep fled from my eyes. These

twenty years I have been in your house; I served you fourteen years for your two daughters and six years for your flock, and you changed my wages ten times. If the God of my father, the God of Abraham, and the fear of Isaac, had not been for me, surely now you would have sent me away empty-handed. God has seen my affliction and the toil of my hands, so He rendered judgment last night'" (31:33-42).

Laban rummaged through the tents of Jacob, Leah, and the two maids but only in vain. Only Rachel's tent remained.

In that suffocating situation, Rachel came up with an idea. She hid the idols under the saddle of the camel and sat on it. Then she lied to her father saying she couldn't stand up because she was in menstruation.

After all, Laban did not find the idols. Rachel must have thought she escaped the crisis with her wisdom, but the matter of fact is that it was by the help of God that Laban was deceived by Rachel's idea.

Laban wouldn't be any less cunning than Rachel. If he had any doubt over Rachel's behavior and searched her, he would have found the idols. But God opened a way out considering Jacob. Here, we should not think God protects us even though we do something untruthful.

God's protection was rendered because it was coherent with the justice. If we just think about Rachel, God couldn't protect her, but God protected the whole family considering Jacob. If

Jacob was aware that the household idols were stolen by Rachel and pretended he did not know, the situation would have been different. God could protect him because he was absolutely not aware that Rachel had stolen them.

Also, if the idols were found, it wouldn't have been just Rachel's personal problem. Laban must have held Jacob responsible, too. But Jacob couldn't be harmed because he had nothing to do with the stolen idols. That is why God could protect him. Now, as Laban could not find the idols even after feeling through everything there, the situation was reversed. He was in a very difficult situation because it meant he wrongfully accused Jacob's family. Now Jacob had a very good opportunity to take the upper hand.

And Jacob wouldn't let go of this chance. Until now, he couldn't really say anything because of the fact that he had run away secretly. But now, as his innocence was revealed, he began to protest strongly saying, "What is my transgression? What is my sin that you have hotly pursued me?" Laban said he wanted to say goodbye to his daughters and grandchildren but Jacob knew Laban's actual intentions. And now Jacob is pointing it out.

Many people take the lower position when they are at disadvantage, but when things change favorably for them, they raise their voice immediately. They suppress their feelings when the situation is disadvantageous for them, but when they get a chance they explode and reveal all the hard feelings they had. Such people will be nice to those who are beneficial to them, but for those who are not, they will neglect them or even be impolite toward them. Also, when they serve those who are higher than they are, they just obey the order and authority and they can't serve from the heart. It was the case with Jacob in that situation.

When Laban caught up with him, Jacob did not humble himself from the heart. He just tried to escape from that disadvantageous situation because he had done something wrong. So, when there was a turn of the events and now he got the upper hand, he immediately raised his voice and revealed his anger. Jacob spoke of all the hard feelings that he had had until then, putting the blame on Laban. He explained how faithfully he worked to take care of the flock of Laban and how much Laban benefitted from him. Furthermore, he reproached Laban saying that had faithfully served him for 14 years to get Leah and Rachel and for another 6 years for the flock and the fact that Laban changed his wages ten times.

Now, he even mentions the name of God in order to protest his rights. He says that God remembered all his hard work and effort for the past 20 years and protected him by appearing in Laban's dream and rebuking him the night before.

We can understand Jacob did not keep quiet about Laban's unfair treatment with a goodness of heart. So, as he didn't want anything more from Laban now and Laban was at disadvantage, he spoke out all his complaints fully. Even though Laban was cunning and cheated Jacob many times, we can see that God couldn't acknowledge Jacob's action as good either.

7. The Treaty between Laban and Jacob

"Then Laban replied to Jacob, 'The daughters are my daughters, and the children are my children, and the flocks are my flocks, and all that you see is mine. But what can I do this day to these my daughters or to their children whom they have borne? So now come, let us make a covenant, you and I, and let it be a witness between you and me.' Then Jacob took a stone and set it up as a pillar. Jacob said to his kinsmen, 'Gather stones.' So they took stones and made a heap, and they ate there by the heap. Now Laban called it Jegar-sahadutha, but Jacob called it Galeed. Laban said, 'This heap is a witness between you and me this day.' Therefore it was named Galeed, and Mizpah, for he said, 'May the LORD watch between you and me when we are absent one from the other. If you mistreat my daughters, or if you take wives besides my daughters, although no man is with us, see, God is witness between you and me.' Laban said to Jacob, 'Behold this heap and behold the pillar which I have set between you and me. This heap

is a witness, and the pillar is a witness that I will not pass by this heap to you for harm, and you will not pass by this heap and this pillar to me, for harm. The God of Abraham and the God of Nahor, the God of their father, judge between us.' So Jacob swore by the fear of his father Isaac. Then Jacob offered a sacrifice on the mountain, and called his kinsmen to the meal; and they ate the meal and spent the night on the mountain. Early in the morning Laban arose, and kissed his sons and his daughters and blessed them. Then Laban departed and returned to his place" (31:43-55).

Laban did not concur with Jacob's protest. Laban also had something to say. He argued that Rachel and Leah, the flock, and everything Jacob had was originally his. He meant to say, "I took you in when you didn't have anywhere to go. I gave you wives and children and I made you rich. You should be grateful."

Both Laban and Jacob argued that they were right without accepting the other's standpoint at all. Nevertheless, Laban would just let Jacob go because he was afraid of God who instructed him to do so in his dream.

But it was not that he really revered God or wanted to follow His will. He still had discomfort. He still wanted to have the upper hand in his relationship with Jacob and he said, "So now come, let us make a covenant, you and I, and let it be a witness between you and me."

Jacob accepted Laban's suggestion and set up a pillar with a stone as a sign of the covenant. He let his kinsmen make a heap of stones, too. Laban called the place "Jegar-sahadutha" meaning that heap was a witness between him and Jacob. In Aramaic it means 'pile of testimony'. Jacob called the place "Galeed" in Hebrew with a similar meaning.

The place Jacob and Laban made a covenant was also called "Mizpah". Mizpah means 'watcher' or 'watch-tower'. This name was given with the hope that God would watch Jacob and Laban as to whether they keep this covenant, even when they were apart from each other.

Laban made Jacob promise before God that he wouldn't mistreat Laban's daughters and he wouldn't take any other wives. He also promised he wouldn't pass this heap to go to harm Jacob, and at the same time he made Jacob promise the same thing before God. We can infer how Laban had been treating Jacob just from this statement of his.

In Laban's view, Jacob was his nephew, the husband of his two daughters, and the father of his grandchildren. And yet, he says neither party will cross the border. He was being very cold as if they were now nobody to each other. He had no love at all.

Laban was heartless, but Jacob's accepting such suggestion was not an act of goodness either in the sight of God. Of course, Jacob left Laban to become independent because God moved his heart to do so. But it doesn't mean Jacob had to sever his connection with Laban completely heartlessly.

What if Jacob and Laban were both good-hearted? They could each take their portions and receive blessings respectively without having to break their relationship off. If they were united and helped each other, they could have grown to become a great power of which other peoples would be afraid.

But they just drew a very clear line and separated. Jacob wouldn't want to go back to Laban. He accepted Laban's suggestion because he thought he wouldn't suffer any loss due to the severed relationship. Neither party had proper heart before God, but at the same time there was great difference between the two in the sight of God. We can see this from the scene in which they made the covenant.

Laban said, "The God of Abraham and the God of Nahor, the God of their father, judge between us." To him, God was just the God of Abraham, Nahor, and their fathers. Of course, he also learned about God from the ancestors, but he didn't revere God as his God who intervened in his life with love.

But Jacob swore by the fear of his father Isaac. It's because, to Jacob, God was not just the God of Abraham his grandfather but also the God of Isaac his father and the God of Jacob himself, who guided him till that day guaranteeing the prayers of Isaac.

Preparing for the Return

Jacob's faith was not just a piece of knowledge in his head. He truly and from his heart believed in and feared God who was alive and working. Also, Jacob offered a sacrifice there and ate with his kinsmen. He believed that the covenant that was sealed before God was guaranteed by Him, unlike a covenant between people that could be broken any time. He wanted to get the acknowledgment of God by offering a sacrifice.

In Jacob's heart was settled the true faith that he had gained through Abraham and Isaac. Although 20 years passed since he left his home, his faith did not change. God chose him and established him as the father of Israel because he had such an unchanging heart.

The next morning, Laban said goodbye to his daughters and grandchildren and went back home. Jacob also set out toward his father's house. But what awaited him was not a welcome, but rather it was very powerful threat to his life. Jacob still had his 'self' left even after being refined for 20 years, and the moment of truth was coming up for him where he had to demolish his ego completely.

Chapter 7

Jacob's Victory in Fierce Spiritual Struggle

Seeing the Angels of God
Jacob's Reconciliation Effort with Esau
Jacob's Supplication in the Face of Crisis
Jacob Still Acts at His Discretion
Thigh Socket Dislocated at Jabbok
Your Name Shall Be Israel

1. Seeing the Angels of God

"Now as Jacob went on his way, the angels of God met him. Jacob said when he saw them, 'This is God's camp.' So he named that place Mahanaim" (32:1-2).

On Jacob's way to Canaan, God briefly showed him what was happening in the spiritual realm. Jacob saw the angels of God. As the angels put on clothes like soldiers, he called them "God's camp." They were angels under the command of Michael who can be likened to the commander of an army.

Why did God open Jacob's eyes and let him see angels? It was to let him know that God was with him and protecting him with His angels. Before allowing important trials for Jacob to demolish his 'self' or ego, God wanted to give comfort and strength to him.

But Jacob did not realize why God had sent His army. He

just thought seeing the army of God was meaningful by itself and called that place "Mahanaim."

And what is the reason the army of God went forward before Jacob? It's because there is always spiritual battle in the process of God's plans being fulfilled.

The crisis that Jacob will face is the struggle with Esau in physical sense. But, in spiritual sense, it was the struggle between God's army and the evil spirits that stand against God. God sent His army so that Jacob could win in this spiritual battle.

If Jacob had been spiritually awake he would have realized the meaning of God showing him His army. Then, he wouldn't have been afraid when he encountered Esau. He could have been bold knowing that God was with him.

Jacob's grandfather Abraham was always spiritually awake, and he always realized the spiritual meaning whenever God did something. Then, he did what he was supposed to do. For example, when he encountered Melchizedek or the angels of God that came down to search the city of Sodom, he knew in his heart exactly what he was supposed to do and put it into action. This difference comes as the result of the extent to which one takes after the heart of God and feels it.

Even though God shows the same thing to two different people, each of them will have a different depth of understanding. The volume of grace each one feels in his heart is also different. Also, the depth of spiritual understanding will be different depending on the extent to which a person is spiritually awake and the fullness of the Holy Spirit.

God opened the spiritual eyes of Jacob and let him see God's army, and yet he could not relate the meaning in it with himself. That is why he couldn't cast away the fear in the reality and he would try to rely on his own wisdom and power. Eventually, a situation occurred in which his 'self' was completely shattered.

2. Jacob's Reconciliation Effort with Esau

"Then Jacob sent messengers before him to his brother Esau in the land of Seir, the country of Edom. He also commanded them saying, 'Thus you shall say to my lord Esau: "Thus says your servant Jacob, 'I have sojourned with Laban, and stayed until now; I have oxen and donkeys and flocks and male and female servants; and I have sent to tell my lord, that I may find favor in your sight.'"' The messengers returned to Jacob, saying, 'We came to your brother Esau, and furthermore he is coming to meet you, and four hundred men are with him'" (32:3-6).

Jacob couldn't help but become afraid of meeting Esau as

long as their previous conflicts were still unresolved. So, he decided to first send his messengers to Esau. He told them what to say to Esau. It is that while he had been with his uncle Laban he had gained many possessions and that he wanted reconciliation.

But Jacob's attitude now was very different from that of the past. 20 years ago, Jacob did not have any respect for his brother Esau. He just exploited Esau's weak points to take the birthright. Also, he cheated his father to take away the blessing intended for Esau.

And yet, he never thought he had done anything wrong to his brother or that it was natural for his brother to get angry. He only justified himself thinking like, 'I bought the birthright for a price. I only followed my mother's instructions to receive the blessing from my father. So, it's not my fault. Also, am I not the one who is supposed to receive the blessing in the first place?'

Had Jacob had his previous attitude, he'd have tried to show off his power coming like a triumphant army general. Or, he might have tried to avoid the anger of his brother just for the moment with his cunning wisdom. But Jacob was very different after going through the trials for 20 years.

As he looked back at the past, he understood Esau could have easily been angry, and he wanted to make it up to Esau. Though he was not sure, he tried to humble himself and find a way to do so. He used his fleshly thoughts rather than relying on God completely, but certainly it was something different from the past that he tried to melt the heart of Esau.

Jacob told the messengers to humbly say to Esau "Your servant Jacob." Saying that he sojourned with Laban was to show to Esau that he had gone through quite an ordeal and humbled himself under Laban.

He hoped that Esau's heart would be appeased to some extent if he heard that his brother went through many sufferings while under his uncle Laban. Jacob said he could give a portion of his wealth to Esau, and asked him to forget the past and forgive him.

Trials can change people. Jacob never respected his brother but only tried to take his things. But now, he humbled himself and even called Esau 'my lord'. He did not use any cunning ways to cheat his brother but only tried to ease Esau's mind in a good way.

That does not mean, however, Jacob had completely changed. He did not refer to Esau 'my lord' with complete regret. Of course, he was sorry to some extent, but he just wanted to find a way to get out of the trouble that he was in.

He did not repent of his wrongdoing thoroughly, and his desire to avoid or get out of the difficult situation was greater than his need to humble himself and completely submit to Esau. If Jacob served Esau with a completely good heart, the situation would have been different. God could have given a solution to the problem very quickly. But that was not the case. God still had to wait for Jacob to completely demolish his ego.

Jacob tried to melt the heart of Esau, but only in vain. The messengers who went to Esau brought back news from him, and there was no hope at all. But rather, they informed Jacob that Esau was coming with 400 men.

3. Jacob's Supplication in the Face of Crisis

"Then Jacob was greatly afraid and distressed; and he divided the people who were with him, and the flocks and the herds and the camels, into two companies; for he said, 'If Esau comes to the one company and attacks it, then the company which is left will escape.' Jacob said, 'O God of my father Abraham and God of my father Isaac, O LORD, who said to me, "Return to your country and to your relatives, and I will prosper you," I am unworthy of all the lovingkindness and of all the faithfulness which You have shown to Your servant; for with my staff only I crossed this Jordan, and now I have become two companies. Deliver me, I pray, from the hand of my brother, from the hand of Esau; for I fear him, that he will come

and attack me and the mothers with the children. For You said, "I will surely prosper you and make your descendants as the sand of the sea, which is too great to be numbered""'" (32:7-12).

After 20 long years Jacob was going back to his home country, but it was not the warm welcome of the family that was awaiting him. It was his brother Esau who was coming toward him with 400 men. Jacob could've lost all his possessions and even his life. He reached his limits; there was nothing else he could do. Now he had to rely on God completely.

Of course, Jacob could choose another way. He couldn't go back because of his treaty with Laban, but he could still go to another place. But he didn't. He didn't give up going back to his home country although Esau was waiting for him, because it was the command of God to go back.

This is one of the most important reasons why Jacob could be chosen by God. Jacob used his wisdom and thoughts, but he never tried to deviate from the will of God. He used some fleshly methods, but his intention was not disobedience. It was just because he still had his own ideas coming out of his 'self'.

Upon hearing the news that his brother Esau was coming toward him with 400 men, he was afraid and felt suffocated. He divided his camels and herds and flock into two groups. If Esau attacked one of them, the other group could run away. He tried to save a portion of his possessions and his life.

Jacob could not commit everything to God from the start. In a dire situation, he began to pray to God only after he did everything he could in his power first.

He prayed, "Deliver me, I pray, from the hand of my brother, from the hand of Esau; for I fear him, that he will come and attack me and the mothers with the children. For You said, 'I will surely prosper you and make your descendants as the sand of the sea, which is too great to be numbered.'"

If he thought his own ideas were perfect and everything would go well, he wouldn't have relied on God. He prayed because he was still afraid even after making all the provisions with his own ideas. Being afraid is the evidence that he did not rely on God and that he still had his 'self'.

He prayed remembering the promise of God given in the past, but it was also a kind of self-centered prayer. He was trying to imply that God had to protect him from the hand of Esau because it was God who had promised to give him blessings in the past. Of course, we have to believe the promises of God and pray about them. But it is not right to ask Him to give us blessings right now only because He had promised blessings in the past.

Then, how should he have prayed? He should have prayed like, "I believe Your promise will be fulfilled in me. Let me realize what I lack to fulfill the covenant. Let me know what I have to do." Namely, he had to pray to change himself and become worthy to receive the blessing while praying for God's promise to be fulfilled as well.

4. Jacob Still Acts at His Discretion

"So he spent the night there. Then he selected from what he had with him a present for his brother Esau: two hundred female goats and twenty male goats, two hundred ewes and twenty rams, thirty milking camels and their colts, forty cows and ten bulls, twenty female donkeys and ten male donkeys. He delivered them into the hand of his servants, every drove by itself, and said to his servants, 'Pass on before me, and put a space between droves.' He commanded the one in front, saying, 'When my brother Esau meets you and asks you, saying, "To whom do you belong, and where are you going, and to whom do these animals in front of you belong?" then you shall say, "These belong to your servant Jacob; it is a present sent to my lord Esau. And behold, he also is behind us."' Then he commanded also the second and the third, and all those who followed the droves, saying, 'After this manner you shall speak to Esau when you find him; and you shall say, "Behold, your servant Jacob also is behind us." For he said, "I will appease him with the present that goes before me. Then afterward I will see his face; perhaps he will accept me"'"

(32:13-20).

After offering the prayer according to his wish, he still utilized his own thoughts. As his previous tactics didn't work, which was to appease Esau by sending his servants, this time he showed his humble attitude once again by sending the livestock. He sent the presents that could please his brother Esau.

Here, we can see what Jacob is like once again. He was still calculating even when his life was at the stake. His offering included more than 500 cows and bulls, sheep, goats, donkeys and camels. They were by no means something small. But it wasn't so much considering the whole possession of Jacob.

What good would his possession be if he was killed by Esau? But even at this dire moment he was willing to give only a portion of his wealth, thinking like, 'What amount of offering will appease Esau?' He was not humbled enough to give himself completely.

Jacob divided the animals into each drove and gave them to his servants saying, "Pass on before me, and put a space between droves." He thought dividing each drove and setting a distance among them was more effective in appeasing Esau, rather than giving him all the gifts at once.

Also, he told his servants, if Esau asked to whom those

animals belonged, to answer, "These belong to your servant Jacob; it is a present sent to my lord Esau. And behold, he also is behind us." He made three droves and instructed the servants to say the same thing.

We can see how meticulous and calculating Jacob is. He made plan B and C as well. It seemed Jacob was relying on God but he was still utilizing his own thoughts and methods.

Of course, it was wise to send the gifts to reconcile with Esau. But the problem is his attitude of heart. If he completely regretted his past actions and sent those presents with a completely humble heart, God could also acknowledge his actions and the problem would've been resolved. But Jacob was not humble enough yet.

Once, Abraham also utilized his thoughts and had to undergo an occasion in which his thoughts were completely demolished. It was when he went down to Egypt in order to escape a famine. He was afraid the Egyptians might kill him to take away his wife who was very beautiful. He asked her to say she was his sister. Ironically, his wife was taken because of his preventive measure. After, it was resolved by God's intervention, but if he had been upfront about his wife, God would have been with him, and his wife wouldn't have been taken.

Through this incident, Abraham thoroughly realized how useless it was to use his own thoughts and methods. Since then, he relied on God only and committed to Him everything.

Jacob went through the trials until then so that his own thoughts could be shattered. Now, the moment of truth was coming up to break his 'self' completely at Jabbok River.

5. Thigh Socket Dislocated at Jabbok

"So the present passed on before him, while he himself spent that night in the camp. Now he arose that same night and took his two wives and his two maids and his eleven children, and crossed the ford of the Jabbok. He took them and sent them across the stream. And he sent across whatever he had. Then Jacob was left alone, and a man wrestled with him until daybreak. When he saw that he had not prevailed against him, he touched the socket of his thigh; so the socket of Jacob's thigh was dislocated while he wrestled with him. Then he said, 'Let me go, for the dawn is breaking.' But he said, 'I will not let you go unless you bless me.' So he said to him, 'What is your name?' And he said, 'Jacob'" (32:21-27).

Jacob sent his presents to appease his brother, and he tried to come up with some ideas to resolve the situation. But he finally realized it was something beyond his own ability. It was the biggest crisis in his life. Only then did Jacob lay down his own wisdom and methods and rely on God.

He arose that night and sent his two wives and his two

maids Zilpah and Bilhah and his eleven children across the Jabbok, and he was left alone. He sent across whatever he had. Why did he do so even before he received any news from his servants?

In order for Jacob, who had been unable to demolish his ego for a long time, to deny himself completely, he needed to be prepared. Namely, he needed time to lay himself down and look back on himself. And God moved his heart to do so. Sending across his wives and children before him means he laid down everything and only relied on God.

Until minutes before, he was trying to find a common ground with Esau and calculating ways to appease him. But he realized his methods were not working at all. Now he realized his wisdom and plans were useless. He laid down his family, possessions, and even his life. He decided to depend on God alone.

When one faces a situation where there is nobody to rely on, when they feel they are completely alone, they then become desperate. Now they turn to God, because He is the only one who can solve the problem and who knows everything. If we lay ourselves down and earnestly seek God, He will not leave us as orphans. He will meet us and answer us. We will be filled when we empty ourselves.

But 'laying oneself down' is not everything. As for Jacob,

to wrestle and win was something more important. In this dire situation, he wrestled with somebody all night. Who was this with whom Jacob wrestled? It was an angel of God. More specifically, it was Archangel Michael.

Michael is the commander of the army of God. His dignity, power, and authority are great and mighty. One might not be able to understand such an archangel couldn't win in the wrestle against Jacob and touched the socket of his thigh and it was dislocated. It does not mean the archangel was defeated by Jacob physically. It tells us what kind of attitude Jacob was clinging to God with.

Jacob knew that the man he was wrestling with was not an ordinary person but an angel of God, who was sent to give him the answer. Jacob had nowhere to turn to but God, and he couldn't let go of this chance.

Jacob had the kind of heart with which he would never give up once he set a goal. Once he kept something in mind, he would never forget. It was at this moment his firm heart is revealed very well. He clung to the archangel Michael all-night with the firm determination that he would never let go or give up.

Having this firm heart and determination is what it means that Michael had not prevailed against Jacob. Namely, Jacob clung to God with a firm and earnest heart, with which he would never give up.

Jacob was in a situation where he could receive God's answer only when he relied on Him with all his life. When God sent His archangel Michael, according to the rules of justice He set the magnitude and amount of faith and effort that Jacob had to show in order for Michael to give him the answer. And, Jacob passed that standard.

Some people say they rely on God, but they set a time limit for God's reply. That is, they pray to God to a certain point in time, but if the answer of God is not given, they just give up or get disheartened. But the timing is decided by God. And what we have to do is just to keep on praying until the answer is given. Jacob did not set this kind of limit but just kept on praying.

Also, archangel Michael touching the socket of Jacob's thigh and dislocating it means Jacob's 'self' or ego was completely destroyed. That was the time when Jacob's self-oriented thoughts, wisdom, methods, and theories were completely broken. His pride, arrogance, and cunningness that he had had until then were also crumbled away.

The thigh is one of the most important parts of the body to support the whole body. In a spiritual sense it means 'uprightness' and 'unchanging heart' and also has to do with the person's authority. Therefore, the thigh is used as a symbol representing one's inner heart or one's unique identity. As for Jacob, this thigh that carries the aforementioned meanings was dislocated.

We can receive answers from God when we break our 'self'. It will also be the moment for us to go into spirit as well as it is the moment for God's answers to come. As Jacob demolished his ego completely, he began to go through various changes.

Toward dawn, archangel Michael said, "Let me go." Jacob replied, "I will not let you go unless you bless me." So he said to him, "What is your name?" As a messenger of God the angel knew everything about Jacob, but he still asked his name to open the way for God's reply to Jacob.

It is something similar with the question of Jesus that He asked a blind man, "What do you want Me to do for you?" Obviously a blind man would want to see. And yet, Jesus still asked him what he wanted, so that he himself would profess his request and the answer could be given in accordance with justice. The blind man answered, "I want to regain my sight," and he received the answer.

If it had been before Jacob was changed, when the archangel Michael asked Jacob, "What is your name?" at Jabbok River, Jacob probably would have wondered why the angel was asking that question and what kind of reply would benefit him the most. But after his 'self' was completely demolished, he did not have any thoughts about it, and like a child he just answered, "Jacob." He received the answer he wanted and the promise of blessing from the archangel Michael.

6. Your Name Shall Be Israel

"He said, 'Your name shall no longer be Jacob, but Israel; for you have striven with God and with men and have prevailed.' Then Jacob asked him and said, 'Please tell me your name.' But he said, 'Why is it that you ask my name?' And he blessed him there. So Jacob named the place Peniel, for he said, 'I have seen God face to face, yet my life has been preserved.' Now the sun rose upon him just as he crossed over Penuel, and he was limping on his thigh. Therefore, to this day the sons of Israel do not eat the sinew of the hip which is on the socket of the thigh, because he touched the socket of Jacob's thigh in the sinew of the hip" (32:28-32).

God renamed Jacob 'Israel'. 'Israel' means 'one who has striven with God and has prevailed.' This means God would fulfill His promise of the blessing of the firstborn given to Jacob through Isaac. As Jacob denied himself completely he was guaranteed the blessings of the firstborn.

So, it means Isaac's blessing would be fulfilled exactly as he said, *"May peoples serve you, and nations bow down to you; be master of your brothers, and may your mother's sons bow down to you. Cursed be those who curse you, and blessed be those who bless you"* (Genesis 27:29).

Once such a blessing is given, Esau would not be able to harm Jacob, and Jacob would be continuously guided to the way of blessings. It also meant God would let Jacob get out of the current difficulty. Jacob received not just the answer to the impending problem but also the word of promise guaranteeing the providence of God that would be fulfilled through him.

As the archangel Michael was giving Jacob his new name Israel, he said, "...for you have striven with God and with men and have prevailed." He said that Jacob prevailed against God while the one Jacob strove with was the archangel Michael.

It's because Michael was the messenger of God who came to bless Jacob in the name of God on God's behalf. Jacob clung to the archangel Michael until he received the answer, and it was the same as clinging to God Himself. "Striving with God and prevailing" also means that Jacob's heart was suitably proper in the sight of God for the answer to be granted. In addition, it also means God chose and used Jacob who had the proper heart in order to establish Israel.

After receiving the new name 'Israel', Jacob asked the archangel Michael what his name was. He did so in order to reconfirm that everything that was happening to him was done in the name of God.

But the archangel Michael replied, "Why is it that you ask my name?" He didn't reply the way he did to ask what Jacob's intention was in asking that question. This means something more like, "How can there be any error in what God is doing, and how wouldn't He fulfill His promise?"

Archangel Michael now blessed Jacob immediately without delay. Jacob named that place where he strove with an angel and prevailed "Peniel." It means 'the face of God'.

No one can see God face to face except those who resemble God completely. Sinners will die upon seeing the face of God. But Jacob knew the one he strove with all-night was an archangel of God, and for this reason he felt like he had seen God face to face.

Here, saying, "I have seen God face to face, yet my life has been preserved" means his prayer was answered after seeing the messenger of God face to face. Jacob received the answer of God but the socket of his thigh was dislocated and he had to limp. It symbolizes that his head wouldn't be held high as in the past when he still had his self-righteousness and self-centered frameworks.

He came to limp and naturally he couldn't hold his head high as the socket of his thigh was dislocated. It means he was completely humbled. Jacob was very tired after striving with the archangel Michael all night long and his thigh bone was dislocated. He was so exhausted that it was hard to just lift a finger.

What could he protest or argue in this situation? He would just say yes to everything with a humble attitude and with thoughts like, 'I am nothing. Let God's will be done.' If the same thing happens to us, we will receive God's blessings. Things will not work out if we try to do things on our own in our own ways, but if we rely on God completely, we will be guided to the way of prosperity.

And for this, we first have to completely deny and humble ourselves. We should not just say with lips we leave everything to God. We have to truly break our ego and 'self' so that we can truly rely on God from the heart and say only 'Yes' and 'Amen'. It's because the evidence of demolishing our 'self' is obedience.

Even though Jacob did not yet possess perfect faith, God's answer came upon him as soon as he crushed his ego. An ordinary person would have given up midway. But Jacob clung to God until he actually received the answer and prevailed after all.

To this day the sons of Israel in remembrance of this event do not eat the sinew of the hip which is on the socket of the thigh of an animal. They want to remember what kind of attitude and heart Jacob had when he received God's blessings. It is also to remember how the nation of Israel started.

This is the kind of heart and character found in no other people. It is uniquely Israel. It is the character they inherited from Jacob. In order to get a nation with upright heart, God chose Jacob, who had the proper inner heart, refined him through trials and established him as the father of Israel.

Meaning of Thigh Bone

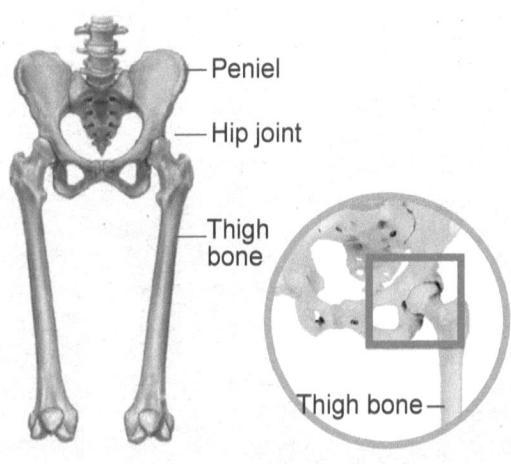

Thigh bone is the longest and strongest bone of all the bones of our body. It is like the pillar that supports the whole weight of the body.

In a spiritual sense, surmounting the meaning of being upright and un-changing in the promise, the thigh bone symbolizes God acknowledges and accomplishes everything. For this reason in the Old Testament times, they made oaths placing their hands under the thigh (Genesis 24:2, 9; 47:29).

Jacob's thigh was dislocated while he was wrestling with an angel. It means the hip joint that connects the pelvis and the thigh bone was in disorder.

The Bible says the angel 'touched the socket of Jacob's thigh'. As his thigh was dislocated and not properly connected with the pelvis, he began to limp. It spiritually shows he came to rely on God completely.

"It's not that I had no regrets at all
at each moment of my life,
but now I thank You, God,
that in Your precious intervention,
You changed me and guided me.
Now You let me beget these many children,
and these children receive blessings of God,
and I give thanks to You.

I want all of them to dwell
in the providence of salvation of God,
and I want them to go their way
in the will of God."

- *Part 2* -

Descendant of Abraham My Friend

Surely I will Help You

/ Part 2 /

Jacob, descendant of Abraham, God's Friend, demolished his ego and changed. He returned to Canaan, received the blessing of the firstborn, and became the father of Israel.

The 12 tribes were formed through his 12 sons. Later, to fulfill the providence of human salvation, Jesus was born as a son of David into the tribe of Judah of Israel.

Jacob
Chapter 8

Back to Canaan after Twenty Years of Trials

Meeting Esau with Boldness and Humbleness
Jacob and Esau Reconciled
Declining Esau's Kindness to Go to Succoth
Reaching Canaan the Land of Promise

1. Meeting Esau with Boldness and Humbleness

"Then Jacob lifted his eyes and looked, and behold, Esau was coming, and four hundred men with him. So he divided the children among Leah and Rachel and the two maids. He put the maids and their children in front, and Leah and her children next, and Rachel and Joseph last. But he himself passed on ahead of them and bowed down to the ground seven times, until he came near to his brother. Then Esau ran to meet him and embraced him, and fell on his neck and kissed him, and they wept" (Genesis 33:1-4).

Jacob experienced the great change in him at Jabbok River. Now, he met with his family that he had sent the night earlier and headed to his home country. Finally he could see Esau and 400 men with him. Jacob received the promise of blessing by striving with the archangel, but in reality the situation didn't seem to have changed. But the biggest change after receiving the promise of blessing can be found in Jacob himself.

Jacob now became bold by relying on God. He divided his family into three groups. He put the maids and their children in the front, Leah and her children next, and Rachel and her child Joseph last.

Just by looking at this scene, it looks like he was making provisions in his own ways with his own wisdom as in the past. Just moments ago he divided his men, sheep, cows and bulls and camels into two groups, so that if one of them got hit by Esau, the other would escape. But this time, there was something different. He stood at the front.

If Jacob had been trying to protect his possessions and life with his own wisdom, he'd have stood at the back. But this time, he stood in the front, willing to give up his life if it came to that. He committed every matter in God's hands and was not afraid of death.

We can see that if he got killed, then probably his concubines and their children would die. Then, if Leah and her children couldn't escape, they might die. But Jacob wanted to save Rachel and Joseph. Does this originate from his favoritism? In a physical sense one might say so, but actually there is a deeper meaning in it. It was to fulfill the providence of God according to the spiritual order.

Jacob wanted to marry Rachel from the start, and the

reason why he served his uncle Laban for 14 years was also to get Rachel as his wife. If Laban had not cunningly given Leah as his wife before Rachel, certainly Rachel would have been his first wife. Therefore, Joseph who was born of Rachel had the birthright in true sense. Joseph was the one to carry on the orthodoxy of the genealogy.

In physical sense, Reuben born of Leah was the first son, but in spiritual sense, Rachel's son Joseph was the first son. That is why through Joseph the way was opened for the family of Israel to go to Egypt and form a big nation.

God considers spiritual order more important than physical order, and He chose Joseph among the 12 sons of Jacob. Though he was not aware of this spiritual providence or spiritual order so clearly, he was moved in his heart to divide the family into three groups by God's urging.

In physical sense also, Jacob had an unchanging heart, and his love for Rachel did not change. So, it is natural that he'd cherish and love Joseph the most, the one to whom Rachel had given birth. This is the reason why he wanted to put Rachel and Joseph at the back to keep them safe. He thought that way perhaps the orthodoxy of his family line would be kept.

After his ego was broken down completely at Jabbok River, Jacob went through many changes in himself. One of them was that he wouldn't try to 'live' but he was willing to die. As soon as he met Esau in the front of his family, he bowed down to the ground seven times. He wasn't just willing to give up his life, but he completely humbled himself as well.

Bowing down to the ground 7 times means he regretted and repented of all his past doings completely as well as he humbled himself completely. He denied himself completely before God, and he wouldn't care about his pride before Esau. He did not think about his wealth or position.

He thought about the standpoint of others first. He came to understand the standpoint and mind of his brother thinking like, 'He must have been really hurt by my actions. If I were in his shoes, I'd have been very angry, too.' He did not give excuses or try to argue he was right. He just understood the heart and viewpoint of his brother.

What kinds of feelings did Esau have at that time? Previously he had burned with anger and he wanted to kill Jacob because his birthright and the blessings had been taken by Jacob 20 years ago. But as time passed, things changed. After Jacob left, he played the role of the first son in his father Isaac's household, and through this situation, his anger was softened.

Then one day, he heard about Jacob's return. His hard feelings rose again to some extent, but he didn't immediately want to kill Jacob. Yes, he was mad thinking about the past, but he thought he'd just ask why Jacob did what he had done in the past. He just wanted to hear Jacob's side of the story.

Meanwhile, his anger subsided even more when he saw the offerings and servants that Jacob sent. He felt Jacob had regrets over the past and that he was willing to serve his older brother.

In this situation, seeing Jacob bowing down to the ground 7 times, all his hard feelings melted away. Esau ran toward Jacob and embraced him and kissed him weeping.

How did Esau's feelings change so very quickly? Of course, it was the work of God. But the basis on which God could do His work was that Jacob was changed.

Jacob was already willing to give up his life, and he truly repented of his past actions from heart. Even if Esau would hurt him, he wouldn't have any resentment or hard feelings about it. As he came to understand the standpoint of his brother, he even had love for him.

The reason why Jacob could go before Esau without fear was because he left everything in God's hands, but also because he had love for his brother.

As 1 John 4:18 says, *"There is no fear in love; but perfect love casts out fear,"* perfect love has no fear. Also, because his ego was completely demolished before God, he laid all his pride, arrogance, and cunningness that he used to have down before Esau. As a result, he could lower himself with the humility stemming from his heart.

As Jacob humbled himself from the depth of his heart, Esau was also moved. He just forgot all the anger and hard feelings he had in the past seeing the true humility of Jacob. Instead of the anger he had only compassion for his younger brother who must have lived a difficult life away from his own family.

As explained already, Esau had such thoughts and mind because God moved his heart. Proverbs 16:7 says, *"When a man's ways are pleasing to the LORD, He makes even his enemies to be at peace with him."* As Jacob was changed to deny himself completely, God heard his prayer and moved Esau's heart to be reconciled with Jacob.

2. Jacob and Esau Reconciled

> *"He lifted his eyes and saw the women and the children, and said, 'Who are these with you?' So he said, 'The children whom God has graciously given your servant.' Then the maids came near with their children, and they bowed down. Leah likewise came near with her children, and they bowed down; and afterward Joseph came near with Rachel, and they bowed down. And he said, 'What do you mean by all this company which I have met?' And he said, 'To find favor in the sight of my lord.' But Esau said, 'I have plenty, my brother; let what you have be your own.' Jacob said, 'No, please, if now I have*

found favor in your sight, then take my present from my hand, for I see your face as one sees the face of God, and you have received me favorably. Please take my gift which has been brought to you, because God has dealt graciously with me and because I have plenty.' Thus he urged him and he took it" (33:5-11).

After weeping together with Jacob, Esau lifted his eyes and saw the women and the children behind Jacob. Supposing they were Jacob's wives and children, he asked with a joyful heart, "Who are these with you?" Jacob's reply was a very wise one. He said, "The children God has graciously given your servant."

This reply pleased Esau. Even though Esau accepted Jacob favorably, he still was a man of flesh. Men of flesh could be very different between when they are filled with the grace of God and when they are not. When they are full of God's grace, they might speak and act like they could understand and forgive anybody, but if they are not filled with God's grace, they might get mad and have hard feelings. Esau, too, could have changed any time by any word Jacob spoke, even though for the moment he was in a good mood.

What if Jacob had said something that could have triggered Esau's hard feelings? For example, if he bragged about his wives and children, saying he received so much blessing from God, Esau's feelings could have been hurt.

Esau thought he was living an affluent life despite the fact that the birthright had been taken by Jacob, and if he realized Jacob was blessed so much, he could have been reminded of the lost birthright. He could have exploded with hot anger remembering that Jacob had taken away the blessings that he was supposed to have received.

But Jacob referred to himself as 'servant' before Esau and just attributed all the blessings to the grace of God. He just humbled himself completely and did not boast of anything. He spoke in a modest manner so Esau would not be provoked in any way.

After Jacob replied, Zilpah and Bilhah brought their sons and bowed before Esau. Next, Leah and her children bowed, and finally, Rachel and Joseph bowed before him.

Jacob was affirming the position of Rachel and Joseph once again by letting them greet Esau last. Rachel is the first wife in spiritual sense, so he treated her and her son Joseph as the head.

Jacob did not just humble himself and bowed before his brother with words and action. He also showed his heart by giving him hearty offerings. Esau asked Jacob about the animals that Jacob had sent as a present. Once again, Jacob with humility replied, "To find favor in the sight of my lord." Seeking favor from his brother means Jacob repented of his past actions thoroughly. Namely, he showed the fruit of his repentance with the offerings. Esau had already accepted the heart of Jacob and he wouldn't want to receive the presents.

Esau had been living a rich life, as the first son of the family. He had possessions that he inherited from his father, and thus he didn't need additional animals. Furthermore, as he had already seen his brother lowering himself completely, he wanted to show some kind of generosity as the one at a higher position. Now, what did Jacob do here?

Did he just withdraw his presents thinking like, 'I expressed my apology, and Esau says he doesn't want it, so I will just take it back'? Surely not! He sincerely wanted to give the present to his brother, and because he had made up his mind to give the present, he had no desire to take it back.

If Jacob had any greed for material things, or if his attitude toward his brother was just formality, he'd have withdrawn the present. But Jacob did not change his mind in this matter and kept on showing his genuine heart.

Moreover, he also wanted to make sure he did actually find favor in his brother's eyes by giving him the offerings. Knowing the spiritual law very well, Jacob wanted to make a clean sheet in his relationship with his brother Esau for that moment.

Jacob went on to say, "I see your face as one sees the face of God." This was not just flattery. Had it been the cunning Jacob in the past, he could have tried to flatter Esau with all kinds of words to soften his heart.

But Jacob was different now. When he said, "I see your face as one sees the face of God," he really meant it, and he meant to say the grace of reconciliation was given by God. He asked Esau once again to accept the presents because he also had enough by the blessing and grace of God.

Esau could not just reject Jacob's sincere gift. All the hard feelings, resentment, and anger melted away, and Esau and Jacob were reconciled with each other.

3. Declining Esau's Kindness to Go To Succoth

"Then Esau said, 'Let us take our journey and go, and I will go before you.' But he said to him, 'My lord knows that the children are frail and that the flocks and herds which are nursing are a care to me. And if they are driven hard one day, all the flocks will die. Please let my lord pass on before his servant, and I will proceed at my leisure, according to the pace of the cattle that are before me and according to the pace of the children, until I come to my lord at Seir.' Esau said, 'Please let me leave with you some of the people who are with me.' But he said, 'What need is there? Let me find favor in the sight of my lord.' So Esau returned that day on his way to Seir. Jacob journeyed to Succoth, and built for himself a house and made booths for his

livestock; therefore the place is named Succoth" (33:12-17).

After this reconciliation in 20 years, Esau suggested to Jacob they go home together. But Jacob with caution declined the suggestion. He respectfully said his children were young and he had a lot of cattle so it was difficult to catch up with Esau.

But of course it was the outward reason. Jacob didn't go with Esau and his men because he knew the heart of men of flesh. Right now, Esau was actually caring for Jacob, but no one at all could guarantee his attitude wouldn't change. He could change his mind any time, if somebody provoked him in any way. Knowing this kind of attribute of fleshly men, Jacob thought it was better they stayed separately and declined the offer.

Jacob had a lot of animals and so did Esau. If they stayed together, they might come across a situation where they wouldn't have enough grass and water to feed their flocks and herds. To keep from developing a rift in their relationship they had to go separate ways.

Of course, Jacob could have spoken as Abraham did to Lot, "If to the left, I will go to the right. If to the right, I'll go to the left." But there could still be a problem. If Esau took the land he thought was better but it turned out it wasn't, then he could have changed his mind and it would have caused trouble.

Fleshly men can change any time, following their own

benefit, even though they have good intention now. Jacob didn't want to take any chances for trouble to arise. It's because he experienced thoroughly how his uncle Laban had mistreated him and that he had changed his wage ten times. The reason why Jacob declined the suggestion of Esau was not because he wanted to serve his own interest. But rather it was for both sides.

Esau agreed, thinking Jacob had a point. They traveled a long distance all the way from Haran, and Jacob's children and the cattle were tired. If they drove the cattle too hard they could also die. Esau couldn't help but accept Jacob's reasoning.

Esau for the last time showed his kindness saying he would leave some of his men to help Jacob, but Jacob declined this offer as well. Why?

It's because they were Esau's men. If things went wrong, even a little bit, they could very well become gossips between Esau and Jacob. Jacob had already experienced such things in Laban's house. Laban's sons said many things with their jealousy toward Jacob. This made Laban angry and eventually Jacob had to run away from Laban.

In the same way, depending on what Esau's men said, the peace that was restored after such a great ordeal could have crumbled in a moment. Knowing such hearts of men, Jacob had to decline this offer as well.

Jacob spoke to Esau as if he was going to follow him soon, but in fact he didn't. There was a reason for it, too. Jacob was the one who would receive the blessing of the firstborn in the will of God. So, if Jacob and Esau stayed together, eventually Jacob was going to receive greater blessings than Esau. What would Esau think if he sees Jacob receive more blessings than he? He'd be reminded of the birthright that had been taken away. He'd develop hard feelings against Jacob again, too.

Also, since Jacob received the blessing of the firstborn, it wouldn't make sense if he stayed under Esau. In physical sense he could serve Esau, but in spiritual sense, Jacob had to be the head, and he couldn't be under his brother. Of course physical order is to be respected but spiritual order is more important.

It might look on the outside that Jacob was utilizing his own wisdom to decline Esau's gesture of kindness every time and to avoid staying with Esau. But unlike in the past, Jacob was being led in the way of prosperity by receiving wisdom of goodness in the grace of God.

Men of God should be more excellent and wiser than unbelievers. I am not talking about just knowledge and education or physical abilities. They can be wiser because they can hear the voice and receive the guidance of the Holy Spirit. When Jacob used to rely on his own wisdom, things never went well. But when he laid himself down and just obeyed the guidance of God, he could be prosperous.

If it had been like that for Jacob in the past, obviously he'd have utilized his own wisdom and experiences. He'd have tried to come up with ways to benefit himself and avoid difficulties. But even though he made a choice based upon his wisdom and past experiences, the difference now laid in his heart.

He did not have any desire to seek his own benefit or do or not do something just to avoid a pressing hardship. He wanted to be guided by God in His plan. As he denied himself and cast away self-oriented desires, he was guided by God even though he still made decisions based on his wisdom and experience.

On that day, Esau went back to Seir. After parting with Esau, Jacob took his family and cattle and arrived at Succoth. Succoth is about 12km north of Adam, at the river mouth of Jabbok. He built for himself a house and made booths for his livestock. He settled in that place. The name Succoth means 'small house'. It is derived from the fact that Jacob built himself a house there.

4. Reaching Canaan the Land of Promise

"Now Jacob came safely to the city of Shechem, which is in the land of Canaan, when he came from Paddan-aram, and camped before the city. He bought the piece of land where he had pitched his

tent from the hand of the sons of Hamor, Shechem's father, for one hundred pieces of money. Then he erected there an altar and called it El-Elohe-Israel" (33:18-20).

From Paddan-aram to Canaan, Jacob's journey was not always smooth, but under God's protection he returned there safely. He left Succoth and arrived at the city Shechem and camped before the city.

Shechem was a city located between Mount Ebal and Mount Gerizim, some scores of kilometers north of Jerusalem. It is the area that Joseph's sons later received as their portion. Joseph's remains were buried there (Joshua 24:32).

Jacob bought the piece of land from the hands of the sons of Hamor, Shechem's father, for one hundred coins. He bought this piece of land to settle there, but big trouble was caused later (Genesis 34).

After he bought the land he followed the example of Abraham. At the site of Shechem, to the oak of Moreh, Abraham received the promise of God saying, "To your descendants I will give this land," and built an altar to the LORD there. Jacob also built an altar. It was in a way to confirm once again he was a descendant of Abraham.

Then he called the altar 'El-Elohe-Israel'. It means 'God is God of Israel'. He put the name he received from God, 'Israel' (Genesis 32:28) to this altar in order to commemorate God who gave him that name.

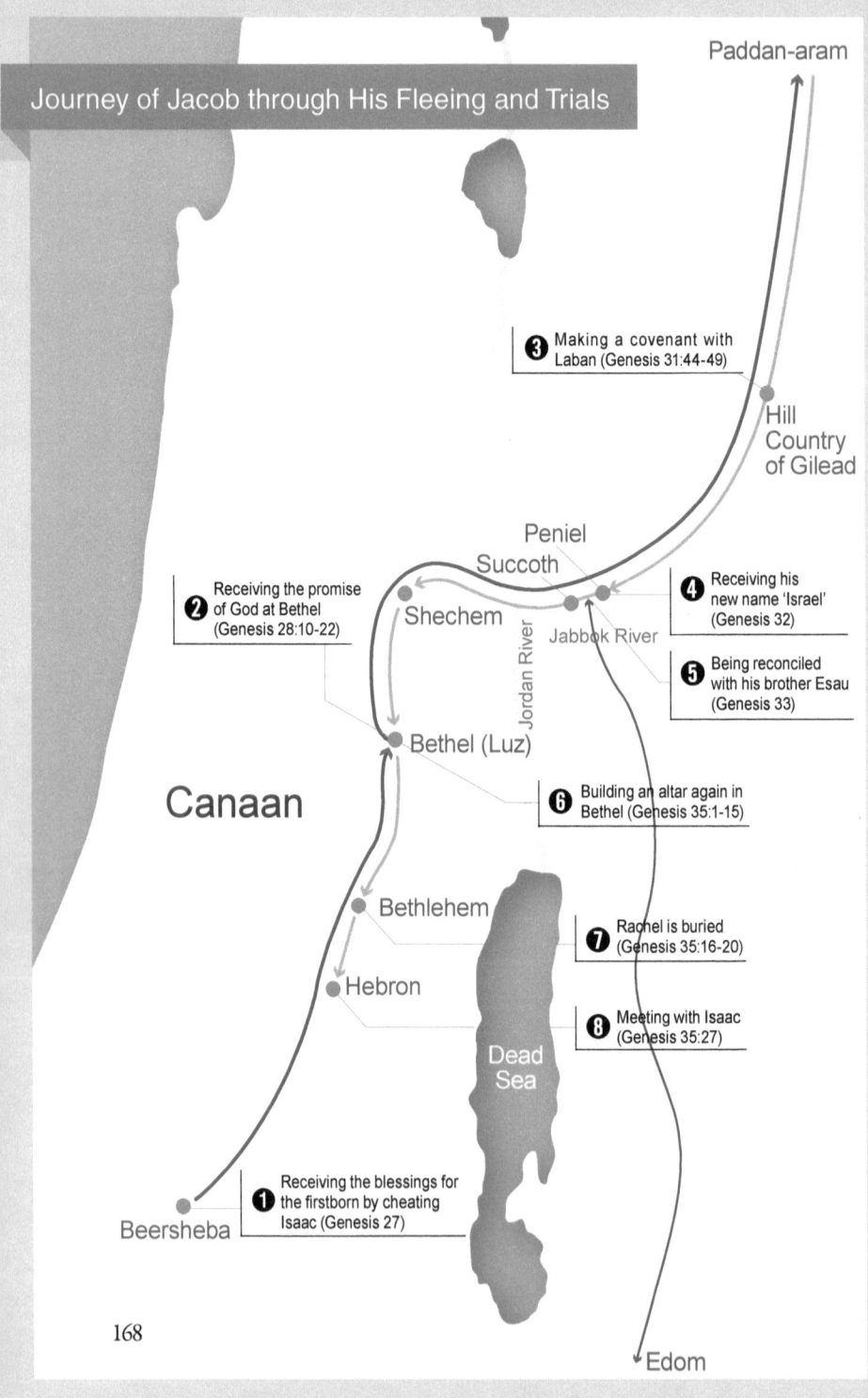

Jacob

Chapter 9

Sin of Simeon and Levi at Shechem

Jacob's Daughter Dinah Suffers Shame

Hamor and Shechem Suggest Marriage

Jacob's Sons Demand Circumcision

Jacob's Sons Pay back Evil with Evil

1. Jacob's Daughter Dinah Suffers Shame

"Now Dinah the daughter of Leah, whom she had borne to Jacob, went out to visit the daughters of the land. When Shechem the son of Hamor the Hivite, the prince of the land, saw her, he took her and lay with her by force. He was deeply attracted to Dinah the daughter of Jacob, and he loved the girl and spoke tenderly to her. So Shechem spoke to his father Hamor, saying, 'Get me this young girl for a wife.' Now Jacob heard that he had defiled Dinah his daughter; but his sons were with his livestock in the field, so Jacob kept silent until they came in. Then Hamor the father of Shechem went out to Jacob to speak with him. Now the sons of Jacob came in from the field when they heard it; and the men were grieved, and they were very angry because he had done a disgraceful thing in Israel by lying with Jacob's daughter, for such a thing ought not to be done" (34:1-7).

So far Jacob's life was not easy. He lived a rough and rugged life. He left his parents and served his uncle for 20 years in Haran. After coming back to Canaan, he had to go through a life-threatening situation.

And a tragedy occurred in Jacob's family once again. It was when Jacob's family was staying in front of the city of Shechem in Canaan. Jacob's daughter Dinah was raped while she went out to visit the daughters of the land. It was by Shechem the son of Hamor the Hivite, the prince of the land.

The Hivites are the descendants of Ham (Genesis 10:17). They are one of the peoples of Canaan that served Gentile gods. Shechem raped Dinah, but he still liked her. So he comforted her and asked his father Hamor to get her as his wife.

We can learn an important lesson from this incident. Why was Dinah not protected by God but had to experience this shame?

Jacob dwelled among the Canaanites, and he must have warned his children about many things they shouldn't be doing there. He must have taught them to avoid following the local customs, worshipping their idols, and marrying the locals there. Especially, to his wives and daughter, he must have prohibited them from coming in contact with anybody there.

But Dinah was curious and she longed for the world. She did not listen to her father, Jacob. She did not just harbor her longing for the world but put it into action, thereby putting herself in a situation that brought about shame.

Lot's wife came out of the city of Sodom that was being destroyed, but she looked back because she couldn't get rid of her clinging attachment to the city. So, she became a pillar of salt. Dinah's case is similar. She went out because of her curiosity for the world, and it caused great pain not just to herself but to her whole family.

Colossians 2:21 tells us about the world: *"Do not handle, do not taste, do not touch!"* But there are some believers who still take the worldly things. It means they are at a halt in spiritual growth. If you feel that your change is slow even though you are striving to cast away sins, you should think about whether or not you are looking at the world or taking in worldly things.

The evidence that Jacob was completely changed at Jabbok is revealed clearly in the incident of Dinah. Jacob heard that Shechem raped his daughter while the sons were tending the livestock in the field. It must have been heartbreaking news, but he kept quiet until the sons came back.

He knew what his sons' reactions would be if they heard the news. He wanted to persuade them after they came back to leave the matter to God and not try to resolve the matter with human methods.

As he expected, the sons were grieved and angry that their

sister was raped. Their reaction was different from that of their father about the same matter.

What would Jacob have done before he was changed? He'd have tried to come up with some ideas and being unable to control his anger he would have hurriedly called for his sons from the field. But Jacob didn't do that.

Even though his daughter suffered great shame, he didn't want to pay back evil with evil. Before he was changed, however, he would have retaliated to even the score. But now, he was not governed by his temper or momentary emotions resulting from the inability to carefully think about all aspects of the situation.

After being in trials for 30 years, Jacob came to carefully think about the results of his actions. Furthermore, now he was the head of the family, responsible for many family members, servants, and a lot of possessions. He couldn't just act on his personal feelings.

Fleshly men are likely to be drawn to their emotions or spur of the moment. They don't usually think about the problems their actions could cause or the pains that other people will suffer due to their actions. Above all, they want to pay back as much as they have suffered. But such an act only brings about more evil.

Romans 12:21 says, *"Do not be overcome by evil, but*

overcome evil with good." True victory is to pay back evil with goodness. Jesus too treated even those who were doing evil to Him and mocking Him, with goodness. The patriarchs also overcame evil with goodness in their lives.

We can also see the heart of fleshly men from Shechem. After defiling Dinah Shechem asked his father to get her to be his wife. This may look like he really loved her and wanted to take her as his wife. Of course, we can say that, because he wanted to take her as his wife, he had at least a bit of conscience; he did not just discard her after raping her.

That does not mean, however, his actions could be justified. Suppose all rapists will be justified if they raped a woman because they loved her. Then, what would happen in the world? If Shechem really loved Dinah and wanted to get her as his wife, he shouldn't have put her to shame. But rather, he'd have upheld her chastity and waited until after he had taken her as his wife in an official wedding.

The same principle can be applied in other areas, too. Suppose you cause pains and deeply hurt the feelings of others. Then, even if you make it up to them, it doesn't mean all your past wrongdoings can be accepted. If you really love somebody, you wouldn't do anything that would hurt them in the first place. If you hurt somebody, first of all, you should thoroughly repent of your fault and ask for forgiveness.

But Shechem and his father Hamor did not do such a thing.

When they came to Jacob to ask him to give his daughter to them, they did not speak a word of apology. Their point was, "Since the situation came to this, just give us your daughter."

In this way, fleshly men do not feel sorry even after hurting others. They just justify their actions thinking 'things happen'. They think that if they try to make up for it, everything is fine.

2. Hamor and Shechem Suggest Marriage

"But Hamor spoke with them, saying, 'The soul of my son Shechem longs for your daughter; please give her to him in marriage. Intermarry with us; give your daughters to us and take our daughters for yourselves. Thus you shall live with us, and the land shall be open before you; live and trade in it and acquire property in it.' Shechem also said to her father and to her brothers, 'If I find favor in your sight, then I will give whatever you say to me. Ask me ever so much bridal payment and gift, and I will give according as you say to me; but give me the girl in marriage'" (34:8-12).

Hamor said to Jacob's sons, "The soul of my son Shechem longs for your daughter; please give her to him in marriage." He also suggested, if they intermarried, the land would be open for Jacob's family.

The Canaanites at that time led a stable life through

farming. So was the case with Hamor and the people of the city of Shechem. On the other hand, Jacob's family was nomadic and they were always on the move. Knowing this fact, Hamor suggested he would help Jacob's family to settle and trade there so they could lead a stable life there.

Shechem also says he'd give anything as the bridal gift if they gave him Dinah. Just by looking at this, it looks like he genuinely loved Dinah. But fleshly men always think about their own benefit and standpoints first.

Even though it looked like they were offering something good to Jacob's family, the fact is they had an ulterior motive. Shechem thought, if he took Dinah as his wife and their families intermarried, all Jacob's possessions would be theirs after all.

That is why Shechem was willing to give anything as the bridal gift. If you have this kind of attitude, you wouldn't remember it when somebody does a favor or shows grace to you. If you paid it back with the same thing or something bigger, you'd think you did what you were supposed to do. Some people even think the one receiving something back from them should be thankful. This is the attitude of fleshly men.

But as for good men, if they have hurt somebody's feelings, they will not stop by doing something nice for them just once. They would ask for forgiveness with a sincere heart until the other's broken heart is melted down, and they will never do the same thing again. Also, if they are shown grace or mercy from somebody else, they will not just pay it back once or twice, but they will keep on repaying the grace continuously. We should be one of such people of goodness in front of God and in front of men.

3. Jacob's Sons Demand Circumcision

"But Jacob's sons answered Shechem and his father Hamor with deceit, because he had defiled Dinah their sister. They said to them, 'We cannot do this thing, to give our sister to one who is uncircumcised, for that would be a disgrace to us. Only on this condition will we consent to you: if you will become like us, in that every male of you be circumcised, then we will give our daughters to you, and we will take your daughters for ourselves, and we will live with you and become one people. But if you will not listen to us to be circumcised, then we will take our daughter and go.' Now their words seemed reasonable to Hamor and Shechem, Hamor's son. The young man did not delay to do the thing, because he was delighted with Jacob's daughter. Now he was more respected than all the household of his father. So Hamor and his son Shechem came to the gate of their city and spoke to the men of their city, saying, 'These men are friendly with us; therefore let them live in the land and trade in it, for behold, the land is large enough for them. Let us take their daughters in marriage, and give our daughters to them. Only on this condition will

the men consent to us to live with us, to become one people: that every male among us be circumcised as they are circumcised. Will not their livestock and their property and all their animals be ours? Only let us consent to them, and they will live with us'" (34:13-23).

Jacob's sons made a suggestion to Shechem and his father who had come to ask for a marriage. They said every man in Shechem had to be circumcised because it is a disgrace to give their daughter to an uncircumcised man.

Circumcision is to cut off the foreskin of a man's penis. Since God commanded it of Abraham, all his children, namely Isaac, Jacob, and their sons were all circumcised on the 8th day of birth. This symbolized that they were in the covenant of God.

Jacob's sons said if every man in the city of Shechem was circumcised, they would intermarry and become one people. On the contrary, if they wouldn't get circumcised, they wouldn't give Dinah to them. But this suggestion was a trick.

They had the hidden goal, which was to kill not just Shechem but also every man in the city of Shechem as a payback. They knew Shechem would persuade all the men in the city to get circumcised in order to marry Dinah. They made a plan to kill every man in the city when they couldn't move freely after the circumcision.

Being unaware of such a plan, Shechem and Hamor thought it was reasonable. Without any hesitation Shechem talked to the people in the city. Because Shechem was more respected than all the household of his father, his words carried weight to the people there.

Hamor and his son Shechem persuaded the people of the city with appealing words. Namely, if they got circumcised, they could intermarry with Jacob's household and become one people, and eventually all the possessions of Jacob would be theirs.

These words were said to persuade the people of the city of Shechem, but it was actually their ulterior motive, too. Shechem did not just genuinely love Dinah. He wanted to take the possessions of Jacob, too.

This is the attitude fleshly men have. On the outside they try to appear as if they are caring for others, but inside they have hidden agenda to fulfill their greed.

4. Jacob's Sons Pay back Evil with Evil

> "All who went out of the gate of his city listened to Hamor and to his son Shechem, and every male was circumcised, all who went out of the gate of his city. Now it came about on the third day, when they were in pain, that two of Jacob's sons, Simeon and Levi, Dinah's

brothers, each took his sword and came upon the city unawares, and killed every male. They killed Hamor and his son Shechem with the edge of the sword, and took Dinah from Shechem's house, and went forth. Jacob's sons came upon the slain and looted the city, because they had defiled their sister. They took their flocks and their herds and their donkeys, and that which was in the city and that which was in the field; and they captured and looted all their wealth and all their little ones and their wives, even all that was in the houses. Then Jacob said to Simeon and Levi, 'You have brought trouble on me by making me odious among the inhabitants of the land, among the Canaanites and the Perizzites; and my men being few in number, they will gather together against me and attack me and I will be destroyed, I and my household.' But they said, 'Should he treat our sister as a harlot?'" (34:24-31)

Thinking about the losses and gains, the men of the city of Shechem agreed to Shechem and Hamor's suggestion to get circumcised. An incident took place on the third day, when the pain was the greatest.

Dinah's brothers who had the same mother as Dinah, Simeon and Levi, took their men and launched a sudden attack on the city. Simeon and Levi killed not only Shechem who defiled Dinah, but also his father Hamor and all other men in the city. The revenge did not end there.

Other sons of Jacob also joined them looting everything

in the city. They took the flocks and herds and other things including women, and even the things in the houses. It was a payback for defiling their sister, but looting everything was great evil.

In the Old Testament times, the common rule was 'an eye for an eye and a tooth for a tooth'. But the reason why God's Law stated it was to warn people to be sensitive about evil and to stop the evil from spreading among the people. It does not mean they could just take revenge to the same extent that they had suffered loss.

Leviticus 19:18 says, *"You shall not take vengeance, nor bear any grudge against the sons of your people, but you shall love your neighbor as yourself; I am the LORD."*

Of course, the Law was not given during Jacob's days. But those who had good hearts and communicated with God followed their good consciences even before the Law had been given.

If something is evil in the sight of God, He will bring judgment in His justice. Romans 12:19 says, *"Never take your own revenge, beloved, but leave room for the wrath of God, for it is written, 'Vengeance is Mine, I will repay,' says the LORD."*

Those who sincerely follow goodness and the truth, will not pay anything back with evil, no matter what kind of evil they suffer. But rather, they will understand others from their heart and accept and forgive them. They overcome with goodness. They will be guided by God through prayers and they will commit everything into the hands of God who governs in justice.

To rely on God who works in goodness and to act in goodness is the way to receive blessings and prosperity (Psalm 37:3). But by killing all men in the city of Shechem through a scheme to take vengeance, they gave the people of the land a reason to take vengeance as well.

Fortunately, God considered Jacob and let fear be upon the neighboring towns so that there wouldn't be any more revenge of blood. This was possible because it was in accordance with justice of God. Namely, Shechem was the one who had committed evil first, and for this reason God put fear in the hearts of the people in the surrounding areas so they wouldn't hurt Jacob's family.

Without this protection of God, Jacob's family wouldn't have been able to survive, for their numbers were small. Of course what Dinah went through was shameful, but if Jacob's sons were good, they'd have followed the will of God and His methods rather than paying back evil with evil at their discretion.

Simeon and Levi took the lead in killing the men of the city of Shechem but other brothers joined them when they were looting the city. Some of them wanted a payback, while the others were just following other brothers.

Now, if you ask those who were just following others, "Why did you do it?" they'd probably say, "It's not that I wanted or planned to do it, but I just happened to follow them."

But it can only be an excuse. If they don't have any desire to participate in such an act, they could never do such a thing. Furthermore, if they actually participated in it, it means they have the same desire in their heart.

Through this incident, Jacob came to have great concern. If the Canaanites and Perizzites heard about what his sons had done and attacked them, the whole family could have been destroyed.

Jacob became afraid after a series of unexpected wicked events in the family. He went up to Bethel to look back on his faith once again, and he carried out the vow he made to God (Genesis 35).

Jacob

Chapter 10

Preparing the Vessel to Receive God's Blessings

Go Up to Bethel and Make an Altar

Religious Reformation of Jacob's Family

The Whole Family Builds an Altar at Bethel

A Nation and a Company of Nations Shall Come from You

Symbol of God's Covenant at Bethel

Benjamin's Birth and Rachel's Death

Leah's First son Reuben and Concubine Bilhah

Jacob Meets His Father Isaac

1. Go Up to Bethel and Make an Altar

"Then God said to Jacob, 'Arise, go up to Bethel and live there, and make an altar there to God, who appeared to you when you fled from your brother Esau'" (35:1).

Jacob's family felt threatened after the annihilation and looting of the city of Shechem. At this moment God told Jacob to go up to Bethel and make an altar there. Bethel is the place where God appeared to Jacob and gave him the word of promise when Jacob was fleeing from Esau to Haran.

At that time, Jacob didn't have anybody to turn to. He was just going to Laban's house without knowing whether he would be accepted or not. He wasn't able to have confidence or assurance, and he didn't have anything with him. But God gave him such an amazing word of promise.

"Your descendants will also be like the dust of the earth,

and you will spread out to the west and to the east and to the north and to the south; and in you and in your descendants shall all the families of the earth be blessed. Behold, I am with you and will keep you wherever you go, and will bring you back to this land; for I will not leave you until I have done what I have promised you" (Genesis 28:14-15).

After a long time, God's promise was being fulfilled through Jacob. God protected Jacob wherever he went and eventually led him to the land He promised. At this point, by reminding Jacob of all the things that happened in the past, God let Jacob understand once again all the blessings came from God.

Of course, Jacob never forgot God's promise during all those years. He never forgot everything was done by God's grace until he was what he had become. Still, God led Jacob to the place where he had met God and received God's promise. It was there he made an altar. This was done by God to reaffirm the covenant and bless him.

The promise of blessing in the past and that now were different in the magnitude of blessing.

When the promise of blessing was given in the past, it was before Jacob was changed. But now, his 'self' was completely destroyed. He was completely renewed. The same word of promise can carry different weight depending on the point in time when the promise is given. In the past, God gave Jacob a promise knowing about the things that would happen to Jacob in the future.

Then, God began to refine Jacob for the next 20 years in Haran so that His covenant could be fulfilled. Now, as Jacob was totally changed and became a vessel worthy to receive blessings, God called him to Bethel once again in order to really bless him.

2. Religious Reformation of Jacob's Family

"So Jacob said to his household and to all who were with him, 'Put away the foreign gods which are among you, and purify yourselves and change your garments; and let us arise and go up to Bethel, and I will make an altar there to God, who answered me in the day of my distress and has been with me wherever I have gone.' So they gave to Jacob all the foreign gods which they had and the rings which were in their ears, and Jacob hid them under the oak which was near Shechem. As they journeyed, there was a great terror upon the cities which were around them, and they did not pursue the sons of Jacob" (35:2-5).

Before Jacob went to Bethel, where God commanded him to go, he made himself and all his family members and servants check their faith again. Namely, he had them throw away foreign gods, purify themselves, and change their garments. Through this reformation he rid his family of idols. One might say in today's terms that he asked those who were with him to all be on the same wavelength.

The covenant which God had given to Jacob could not be fulfilled just by Jacob's efforts alone. Yes, Jacob all by himself could be protected and blessed by God, but for the nation of Israel to be formed through him, all his family had to be fully conformed to follow the will of God.

If anybody in the family was unrighteous or going against the will of God, then the blessings couldn't come. Knowing this fact very well, he checked a couple of things before he went to God and made an altar.

First, he said, "Put away the foreign gods which are among you." This means that we have to cut off the worldly things. Namely, if we love something more than God we have to get rid of it. Also, even if we do not love something more than God, as long as it distracts our attention away from God, we have to cast it off as well.

1 John 2:15 says, *"Do not love the world nor the things in the world. If anyone loves the world, the love of the Father is not in him."* World is the generic term for everything that is opposite of God who is Light. If we love the worldly things, sin will come into us, and if we keep on committing sins, we

will eventually face death, which is the wage of sin (Romans 6:23).

Therefore, God tells us to cast away the world that is embedded in our hearts and mind, and eyes and ears and body. If we cut off the worldly things completely, God's grace will come upon us and we will have confidence in our heart. Thus, we will be able to receive whatever we ask in prayer.

Second, Jacob said, "Purify yourselves and change your garments." 'Purify' here means the action of outward purification. In the Old Testament times, before the Holy Spirit came to people, it was an era of faith in action. Therefore, they had to purify themselves outwardly when they were going before God. But what is more important is the holiness of the heart. That is why Jacob told them to change their garments.

'Garments' refers to 'heart' in a spiritual sense. We have to take off the garment we used to wear and change into a new garment. Namely, we have to take off the previous heart that is filthy and smells foul, and change it into a holy and beautiful heart of the truth (Ephesians 4:22-24). God will certainly give us the answers and blessings if we go before God after changing our garments in this way.

Third, he hid the foreign gods and rings under the oak. By the instruction of Jacob everyone in the household gave the foreign gods and earrings they had to Jacob. The foreign gods symbolize 'all the old habits and sinful things that the former being had'. 'Rings' is the symbol of a slave, meaning one belongs to somebody spiritually.

The rings among the gentiles were not just ornaments but they were related with idolatry. Various images were etched in the rings, and these images naturally became idols. Some people believed these rings had some magical power. Therefore, to throw away rings means they were leaving idolatry and at the same time they were being set free from the slavery to the enemy devil and Satan.

Jacob's hiding the foreign gods and rings under the oak means he destroyed them completely so that people wouldn't look for them again. This means coming out from the darkness and going toward God who is Light. This is the kind of attitude that believers, who are going before God, should have.

The 'oak' symbolizes faith. Therefore, 'hiding it under the oak' means 'hiding it with faith'. Abraham, too, built an altar near the oak when he was making an altar before God. When he offered his sacrifices under the oak, it means he relied on God with faith seeing each of the acorns on the tree.

Jacob set out for Bethel only after he finished preparations to build an altar. Now, he had another concern. It was a concern about the possible retaliation of the Canaanites and Perizzites for what Jacob's sons had done to the men in the city of Shechem. Shechem was the one who first did an evil thing, but Jacob had to be worried because his sons paid the evil back with evil.

Fortunately, by God's protection Jacob's family was not harmed. It was possible because it was in accordance with God's justice. Although Dinah suffered a great shame, Jacob did not pay it back with evil but just intended to leave it to God. Furthermore, he was completely unaware of his sons' plan to attack the city of Shechem. Because the sons had done it at their discretion, Satan could not accuse Jacob.

God let there be a great terror upon the cities which were around them, and they did not pursue Jacob and his sons who were headed to Bethel. This was God's grace protecting Jacob. But the retribution for the evil deed of his sons fell upon them at a later time.

3. The Whole Family Builds an Altar at Bethel

"So Jacob came to Luz (that is, Bethel), which is in the land of Canaan, he and all the people who were with him. He built an altar there, and called the place El-bethel, because there God had revealed Himself to him when he fled from his brother. Now Deborah, Rebekah's nurse, died, and she was buried below Bethel under the

oak; it was named Allon-bacuth" (35:6-8).

Jacob's people arrived at Bethel safely. Jacob kept his promise to God by building an altar there, and he called the place 'El-bethel'. It means 'God of Bethel'. We can understand two things here.

First, it is that everyone who was with Jacob went to Bethel together. They all obeyed Jacob's command to throw away foreign gods and to purify themselves. As a result, every single person could participate in the building of an altar to God.

Second, Jacob built an altar in accordance with God's will. The reason why God called Jacob to Bethel again was to let him remember, commemorate, and give thanks for the time when God had appeared to him and blessed him when he was fleeing from his brother Esau, by building the altar. Jacob accurately understood the meaning about building the altar and obeyed God's will.

Today, some worship services or church events deviate from the proper purposes. The purpose of all worship services, meetings, and other events must be for giving glory to God.

But some believers have meetings or events in the church not for the glory of God but for their own satisfaction or even for monetary gain. God will pleasingly accept worship services, meetings, and events only when we gather and offer those meetings to God in accordance with the actual purposes.

Among Jacob's people was Deborah, Rebekah's nurse. Ever since she had left Paddan-aram along with Rebekah (Genesis 24:59), she had been with Rebekah all the time. After Rebekah died, she dwelled in Jacob's house. Now this Deborah died.

Jacob buried her under the oak below Bethel and called the place 'Allon-bacuth'. It means 'The oak of mourning'. We can see Jacob's tremendous sorrow over losing Deborah.

Deborah's death did not spiritually have noteworthy significance. But the records about it let us know about their culture: having a nurse and burying the dead under a tree. Also, it does not just say she was buried under any random tree, but it says the exact location and even the name of the tree. It tells us all the records in the Bible are historical facts.

4. A Nation and a Company of Nations Shall Come from You

"Then God appeared to Jacob again when he came from Paddan-aram, and He blessed him. God said to him, 'Your name is Jacob; you shall no longer be called Jacob, but Israel shall be your name.' Thus He called him Israel. God also said to him, 'I am God Almighty; be fruitful and multiply; a nation and a company of nations shall come from you, and kings shall come forth from you. The land which I gave to Abraham and Isaac, I will give it to you, and I will give the land to

your descendants after you.' Then God went up from him in the place where He had spoken with him" (35:9-13).

As Jacob made an altar and prayed, God blessed him and once again and confirmed that his name is Israel. God had already given Jacob his new name Israel in Peniel (Genesis 32:28), and He reconfirmed it in Bethel.

God named Jacob Israel to establish him as the foundation of the people of Israel and fulfill His covenant. Because this event carried significant meaning, it says God appeared to Jacob again and blessed him.

God went up from Jacob after giving him the word of blessing. Just this verse alone sounds like God appeared to Jacob in person and then went back up to Heaven.

Also, when God told Jacob to go to Bethel and make an altar, Genesis 35:1 says, "Then God said to Jacob," so it looks like God appeared before Jacob in person. But in neither case did God appear before Jacob in person. Men cannot speak to God face to face.

Speaking to God face to face was allowed only to a very special person like Moses who was meeker and more humble than anybody and who was faithful in all God's household (Numbers 12:3-8). But Jacob was not perfect enough to be able to speak to God face to face. He simply was not qualified to see the image of God. Therefore, he couldn't speak to God face to face or see the image of God.

And yet, the Bible writes as if God appeared and spoke to Jacob in person. But it was that God spoke to him in his heart and he heard His voice from within.

In today's sense, which is the era of the Holy Spirit, it is same as God letting us hear the voice of the Holy Spirit. In the Old Testament times, the Holy Spirit did not dwell in the hearts of men, but He still worked in various ways.

For example, 2 Chronicles 28:11-12 (KJV) says, *"…And the pattern of all that he had by the spirit, of the courts of the house of the LORD, and of all the chambers round about, of the treasuries of the house of God, and of the treasuries of the dedicated things."* It means the Holy Spirit taught David the plan and pattern of the Temple.

After Jacob was changed into the truth, he could hear the voice of God coming from within his heart. Even though it was just from his heart, it was still the voice of God and that is why it says God spoke to him.

5. Symbol of God's Covenant at Bethel

"Jacob set up a pillar in the place where He had spoken with him, a pillar of stone, and he poured out a drink offering on it; he also

poured oil on it. So Jacob named the place where God had spoken with him, Bethel" (35:14-15).

Jacob set up a pillar in the place where He had spoken with him, a pillar of stone, and he poured out a drink offering on it. A drink offering is usually wine. After pouring the drink offering, he poured oil on it and named the place Bethel. Jacob wanted to set up a symbol of the covenant that he had received from God.

Setting up a pillar of stone means God will lay the foundation of Israel through Jacob as He had spoken, because the word of God never changes. Pouring the drink offering and oil on it means the covenant cannot be reverted. God's promise was yet to be fulfilled, and yet, Jacob did not have a shred of doubt about the fulfillment of God's covenant. And through this act of faith, he wanted to reaffirm the covenant.

Of course, God is faithful and His promises are certainly fulfilled. But Jacob made his trust with God more solid by setting up the pillar of stone and pouring the drink offering and oil on it. And before such an act of faith, God had no choice but to carry out His promise completely.

Suppose you will certainly keep your promise that you made to others. You will do what you have said, but there still is a difference between whether or not the people show some kind of evidence of their trust in you. The same goes for our relationship with God. The situation of showing our deeds of faith before God and not doing it are quite different from each other.

6. Benjamin's Birth and Rachel's Death

> *"Then they journeyed from Bethel; and when there was still some distance to go to Ephrath, Rachel began to give birth and she suffered severe labor. When she was in severe labor the midwife said to her, 'Do not fear, for now you have another son.' It came about as her soul was departing (for she died), that she named him Ben-oni; but his father called him Benjamin. So Rachel died and was buried on the way to Ephrath (that is, Bethlehem). Jacob set up a pillar over her grave; that is the pillar of Rachel's grave to this day"* (35:16-20).

After the setting up of the pillar of stone as symbol of covenant in Bethel, Jacob and his people journeyed from there. They reached a place near Ephrath, and something sorrowful happened to Jacob. Rachel died after severe labor. The child was the second son of Rachel and the last son of Jacob.

Rachel felt she was dying and she named her son Ben-oni, which means 'my son of sorrow'. Being in mourning, Jacob could not call him that, and he named him Benjamin, meaning 'son of the right hand'.

Rachel was a very big part of Jacob's life. He had three more wives in addition to Rachel, but it was only Rachel Jacob really wanted. His love for her never changed. Yes, quite a few problems were caused by Rachel's jealousy, but Jacob's love remained unwavering.

If our love for a certain person cools down from a certain moment just because their thoughts are different or they are giving us a hard time, then it is not true love. True love is to understand and accept others in any situation and to continually give our heart without change. In this sense, Jacob truly loved Rachel, and she was comfort to Jacob throughout his life.

Therefore, Jacob's sorrow after losing Rachel had to be tremendous. We cannot attribute her death only to lack of medical care at that time. She could have given birth easily if God protected her. Now, what is the reason that she couldn't live long?

As mentioned, Rachel had a serious problem with jealousy. This is also the main reason why she couldn't conceive a child for a long time. She gave birth to Joseph a very long time after the wedding, but still it was by God's grace given in consideration of Jacob.

Even after she had a son she wasn't satisfied and she still had a lot of jealousy. We can understand this from the fact that she named her son Joseph, which means "May the LORD give me another son." She was certainly loved the most by her husband, and yet rather than changing her undesirable attitude, she just kept on piling jealousy upon jealousy. Eventually, she couldn't be protected by God because of the evil that she had stored up, and she died in childbirth.

So, Rachel could not live long due to her evil, and was she still saved? We cannot say she circumcised her heart or served God very well from her heart, but all the time she was with Jacob she was there in the place of serving and worshiping God.

When Jacob was making altars before God, she worshipped God and kept the statutes together with him. Even though it was not completely out of her volition that she believed and served God, it is still the case that she did follow the statutes of God.

So, considering the fact that it was the time when they were saved according to their deeds, we can say she at least had the faith to be saved. Jacob buried Rachel at Ephrath and set up a gravestone before he continued on his journey.

Jacob's sorrow was great after losing his beloved wife Rachel. Especially, he must have been heartbroken seeing the newborn baby Benjamin who was born without his mother and the little Joseph. Such pity later became favoritism for him which caused jealousy among the brothers.

7. Leah's First son Reuben and Concubine Bilhah

> "Then Israel journeyed on and pitched his tent beyond the tower of Eder. It came about while Israel was dwelling in that land, that Reuben went and lay with Bilhah his father's concubine, and Israel heard of it. Now there were twelve sons of Jacob the sons of Leah: Reuben, Jacob's firstborn, then Simeon and Levi and Judah and Issachar and Zebulun; the sons of Rachel: Joseph and Benjamin; and the sons of Bilhah, Rachel's maid: Dan and Naphtali; and the sons of Zilpah, Leah's maid: Gad and Asher. These are the sons of Jacob who were born to him in Paddan-aram" (35:21-26).

Jacob and his people pitched their tent beyond the tower of Eder on their way back to Hebron. While Jacob was still in mourning for his deceased wife Rachel, he had to hear such shocking news. The first son, Reuben, born of Leah had laid with Bilhah the father's concubine.

Bilhah was a maid of Rachel who later became Jacob's concubine. And Bilhah and Reuben deserved to be put to death for their sin. But Jacob did not get angry or tell anyone about it. He just kept quiet and gave them a chance to resolve the situation by themselves.

If it had been the Jacob before he changed, he'd have revealed their sin and punished them. But Jacob didn't. Rather than taking care of the matter himself, he just left it to God and hoped God's will would be done.

As he had gone through a long period of trials, he cultivated goodness and love with which he could cover other people's iniquities with gentleness of heart and wait for them with a peaceful heart. Of course, in the view of justice, he should have taken strict actions toward Reuben and Bilhah. But what would have happened if he had?

If he punished them sternly or drove one of them out, there would be no more sins. But the punishment would have little meaning if they didn't repent of their sin from the heart. The punishment could have been an example to others, so they wouldn't commit the same sin. But Reuben and Bilhah wouldn't get a chance to repent and they would fall into eternal death.

What if Jacob called them in and rebuked them sternly? It would turn out to be a good idea if they truly repented and turned from their ways, but if they just pretended to be regretful, it'd be useless. They could commit the same sin again.

Jacob wanted them to repent and turn from their hearts. That is why he did not reveal their sin or punish them. He just explained to them so they'd understand; he waited for them to repent on their own. This is the kind of love that transcends justice. Jacob's actions here show to us that he came to have the heart of God after going through all the trials.

Through this incident Jacob once again pondered over the futility of life. Also, it was a chance for him to solidify his willingness to commit everything to God. It was surely an enraging incident, but he passed it with the goodness of his heart, and it became spiritual blessing for him.

Jacob had six sons from Leah, Joseph and Benjamin from Rachel, and four other sons from two concubines. Among these 12, everyone but Benjamin was born in Paddan-aram. Now, the era of Jacob was passing and the era of the sons was coming up.

8. Jacob Meets His Father Isaac

> *"Jacob came to his father Isaac at Mamre of Kiriath-arba (that is, Hebron), where Abraham and Isaac had sojourned. Now the days of Isaac were one hundred and eighty years. Isaac breathed his last and died and was gathered to his people, an old man of ripe age; and his sons Esau and Jacob buried him"* (35:27-29).

Jacob's actions after coming back to Canaan from Haran, from his uncle Laban, raise a question. He did not immediately go to meet his father Isaac after the reconciliation with Esau.

It'd be a son's duty to go to see his father as soon as possible. Isaac must have heard about Jacob's return and eagerly waited for him. But Jacob spent a while after settling down at

Shechem.

Jacob went to Hebron to meet his father only after Dinah's incident. There was a reason for it. Esau and Jacob reconciled, but there still remained the problem of the birthright.

What if Jacob reconciled with his brother and went to meet his father right away? Isaac probably would have welcomed Jacob and celebrated his return since he had received a lost son back.

If Esau had witnessed such a scene, his emotions would have been stirred. If he felt Isaac welcomed Jacob more than he had expected, he could change his mind any time. That is why Jacob put a hold on going to see his father. He waited until the time was right in order to maintain peace with his brother.

After all the trials, Jacob did not decide the timing to act at his discretion but he received the urging of God in his heart. He also missed his father whom he had not seen for 20 years. By showing him his success he wanted to make up for all the disrespect he had showed in the past. And yet, he just patiently waited for the right time.

As Jacob passed the time, Esau's guard against Jacob was lowered even more. He did not consider Jacob to be a threat to his birthright any longer.

Only then, by the inspiration he received from God, did Jacob go to Isaac. What we have to understand is that everything was done with the most appropriate timing. Because

God controlled it all, Isaac could breathe his last in peace after meeting with Jacob and then the whole family had peace.

What if Jacob was a little late and went to Hebron after Isaac died? How regretful he would have felt! He only caused worries for his father, and if he couldn't show any of his success to his father and if he couldn't even see his father before the last moment, how could he have had peace of mind? And as for Isaac, too, he wouldn't have been able to breathe his last in peace if he hadn't seen Jacob.

But as Jacob acted according to the urging of God, everything was done beautifully, without anybody having any regret or hurt feelings. God caused all things to work for the good in peace. Isaac finally lost all his energy and his life ended at the age of 180. Esau and Jacob buried their father in the cave in the field of Machpelah which was before Mamre (Genesis 49:29-31).

The field of Machpelah was a piece of land that Abraham bought from Ephron with 400 shekels of silver. This land was the first that Abraham possessed in the land of Canaan, which God had promised to give to Abraham and his descendants (Genesis 13:15, 17:8). It symbolizes the Canaan Land as a whole that would be given to the sons of Israel later.

Until God's promise to Abraham was fulfilled, the cave of Machpelah always reminded Abraham's descendants of the fact that Canaan was the Promised Land of God. Abraham, Sarah, and Rebekah were buried there. Now, Isaac too was buried there. Later, Leah, and Jacob would also be buried there. It was the family graveyard for Abraham and his family.

Jacob
Chapter 11

Esau's Family Leaves Canaan

Esau's Family Dwells in Seir
Genealogy of Edom's Children and Chiefs
Kings of Edom and Chiefs Thereafter

1. Esau's Family Dwells in Seir

"Now these are the records of the generations of Esau (that is, Edom). Esau took his wives from the daughters of Canaan: Adah the daughter of Elon the Hittite, and Oholibamah the daughter of Anah and the granddaughter of Zibeon the Hivite; also Basemath, Ishmael's daughter, the sister of Nebaioth. Adah bore Eliphaz to Esau, and Basemath bore Reuel, and Oholibamah bore Jeush and Jalam and Korah. These are the sons of Esau who were born to him in the land of Canaan. Then Esau took his wives and his sons and his daughters and all his household, and his livestock and all his cattle and all his goods which he had acquired in the land of Canaan, and went to another land away from his brother Jacob. For their property had become too great for them to live together, and the land where they sojourned could not sustain them because of their livestock. So Esau lived in the hill country of Seir; Esau is Edom" (36:1-8).

Esau did not consider the birthright important. He did not keep the word of God in his mind either. He easily said he'd sell the birthright for a bowl of lentil stew. He also took a Gentile wife for himself.

If he had a clear sense that he is the firstborn, he'd have definitely taken a wife from among his own people. But as his wives he got Adah the daughter of Elon the Hittite, and Oholibamah the daughter of Anah. They were Canaanites who deeply indulged themselves in idolatry.

It was only after a while he realized that taking gentile wives was a threat against receiving the blessings of the first son. So, he married Basemath, Ishmael's daughter. He begot 5 sons from 3 wives.

Later Esau once again showed that he did not keep the word of God in mind. He left the land that God promised to give to Abraham, where he was living with his father Isaac, and moved to a place that looked good to him. It in essence means he gave up the right of the firstborn by going to another place.

One might think Esau yielded the place to Jacob because the possessions of Esau and Jacob were so much that they couldn't stay together. After all, Esau's departure led Jacob to receive the blessing of inheriting the land promised by God with legitimacy. And as for Esau, it proves that he did not understand the meaning, responsibility, and rights of the firstborn.

The nominal birthright is not important. One must keep the land that God promised and receive God's guidance in order to become the actual first son. Esau was missing this point. Esau took all his household and possessions and moved to the hill country of Seir. It is mountainous area south of the Dead Sea. It was a land where Horites were living.

2. Genealogy of Edom's Children and Chiefs

"These then are the records of the generations of Esau the father of the Edomites in the hill country of Seir. These are the names of Esau's sons: Eliphaz the son of Esau's wife Adah, Reuel the son of Esau's wife Basemath. The sons of Eliphaz were Teman, Omar, Zepho and Gatam and Kenaz. Timna was a concubine of Esau's son Eliphaz and she bore Amalek to Eliphaz. These are the sons of Esau's wife Adah. These are the sons of Reuel: Nahath and Zerah, Shammah and Mizzah. These were the sons of Esau's wife Basemath. These were the sons of Esau's wife Oholibamah, the daughter of Anah and the granddaughter of Zibeon: she bore to Esau, Jeush and Jalam and Korah. These are the chiefs of the sons of Esau. The sons of Eliphaz, the firstborn of Esau, are chief Teman, chief Omar, chief Zepho, chief Kenaz, chief Korah, chief Gatam, chief Amalek. These are the chiefs descended from Eliphaz in the land of Edom; these are the sons of Adah. These are the sons of Reuel, Esau's son: chief Nahath, chief

Genealogy of Esau in Genesis 36

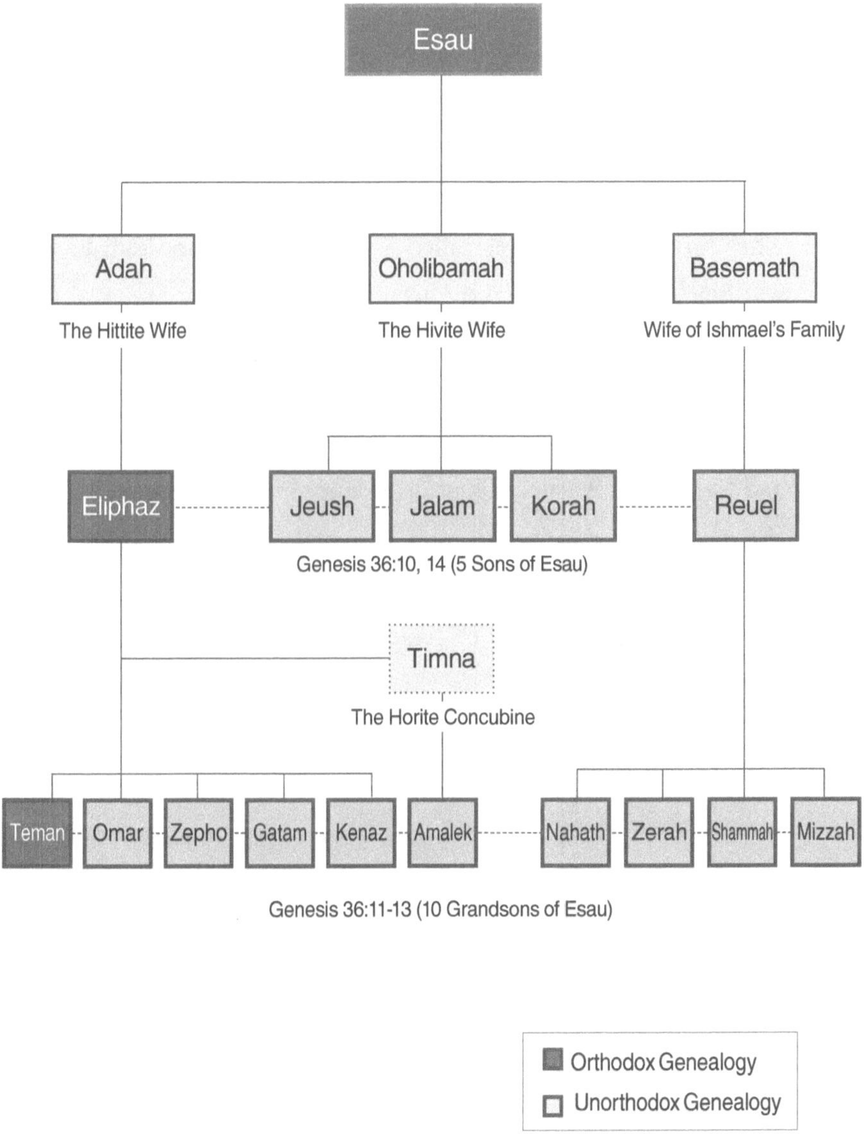

```
                          Esau
        ┌──────────────────┼──────────────────┐
      Adah            Oholibamah           Basemath
  The Hittite Wife   The Hivite Wife   Wife of Ishmael's Family
        │            ┌─────┼─────┐            │
     Eliphaz ----- Jeush  Jalam  Korah ----- Reuel
                  Genesis 36:10, 14 (5 Sons of Esau)

                        Timna
                  The Horite Concubine

  Teman-Omar-Zepho-Gatam-Kenaz-Amalek   Nahath-Zerah-Shammah-Mizzah
              Genesis 36:11-13 (10 Grandsons of Esau)
```

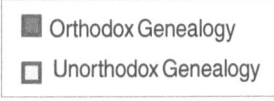

■ Orthodox Genealogy
□ Unorthodox Genealogy

Zerah, chief Shammah, chief Mizzah. These are the chiefs descended from Reuel in the land of Edom; these are the sons of Esau's wife Basemath. These are the sons of Esau's wife Oholibamah: chief Jeush, chief Jalam, chief Korah. These are the chiefs descended from Esau's wife Oholibamah, the daughter of Anah. These are the sons of Esau (that is, Edom), and these are their chiefs" (36:9-19).

The sons of Esau defeated the Horites and settled there. They formed a big people called Edom. Edom means 'red'. It was Esau's nickname given for his red skin, and it also refers to his descendants.

Esau's Hittite wife Adah gave birth to Eliphaz. He was the first son. Eliphaz's sons were Teman, Omar, Zepho and Gatam and Kenaz, and Amalek. They all became chiefs. Among them, the most important one would be Amalek, whom Eliphaz begot from his Horite concubine Timna.

Later, when the sons of Israel who came out of Egypt were passing the wilderness, the Amalekites attacked them at Rephidim in a very underhanded way. They attacked the stragglers at the rear, especially the faint and weary. God swore He would have war against Amalek generation to generation (Exodus 17:16). He also said never to forget what Amalek did and to blot out the memory of Amalek from under heaven (Deuteronomy 25:17-19).

Esau's wife Basemath, who was from Ishmael's family,

gave birth to Reuel. Reuel gave birth to Nahath and Zerah, Shammah and Mizzah. Esau's wife Oholibamah, the daughter of Anah and the granddaughter of Zibeon: she bore to Esau, Jeush and Jalam and Korah. They were the chiefs of the sons of Esau.

Esau at his discretion went to an area where the Gentiles lived. But after generations his sons formed the great kingdom of Edom. Just as God let the sons of Ishmael multiply considering Abraham, He also showed grace to Esau for he is also the son of Isaac and grandson of Abraham.

Esau's sons, the Edomites intermarried with the people of the hill country of Seir, and they became Gentiles who had no relationship with God. They couldn't be the elect, the chosen people of God who would be at the center of the history. They were used just as instruments in human cultivation as a neighbor of Israel.

And this was the result of their own choice. The blessing for the first son went to Jacob, and the sons of Israel would be God's elect. If, however, Esau and his sons had not departed from God, God's blessing wouldn't have left them. They'd have enjoyed the blessings together with Israel as a brother nation that served God.

But they left God and fell into the flesh. Eventually they were severed from God. Esau and his descendants forsook

God's blessings by departing from Him. For this reason, knowing everything about the future, God had to choose Jacob and not Esau as the father of God's elect, Israel.

If we really long for God's blessings our priority should not be material blessings. The most important blessing is salvation and then spiritual blessings that God's children can enjoy. If we receive spiritual blessings, our souls will prosper. All the other blessings in the family, workplace, or the business will naturally follow.

Some people seek material blessings first, without understanding the importance of spiritual blessings. Rather than caring about loving God and receiving His love by sanctifying their hearts, they are more prone to seek fleshly things such as money or fame, being drawn by their greed.

They try to do different things within their own plans, and when things don't work out the way they've hoped them to, some of them leave God. These people do not understand what is really important. They are like Esau who sold his birthright for a bowl of lentil stew (Hebrews 12:16).

Or, as for some people, after they receive material blessings by God's grace, they become rich in heart, which means they've become spiritually lazy. Therefore, in order for us to receive true blessings, we should become like newborn babies in spirit and long for the pure milk of the word (1 Peter 2:2), so that we can receive true blessings both in spirit and in body.

3. Kings of Edom and Chiefs Thereafter

"These are the sons of Seir the Horite, the inhabitants of the land: Lotan and Shobal and Zibeon and Anah, and Dishon and Ezer and Dishan. These are the chiefs descended from the Horites, the sons of Seir in the land of Edom. The sons of Lotan were Hori and Hemam; and Lotan's sister was Timna. These are the sons of Shobal: Alvan and Manahath and Ebal, Shepho and Onam. These are the sons of Zibeon: Aiah and Anah he is the Anah who found the hot springs in the wilderness when he was pasturing the donkeys of his father Zibeon. These are the children of Anah: Dishon, and Oholibamah, the daughter of Anah. These are the sons of Dishon: Hemdan and Eshban and Ithran and Cheran. These are the sons of Ezer: Bilhan and Zaavan and Akan. These are the sons of Dishan: Uz and Aran. These are the chiefs descended from the Horites: chief Lotan, chief Shobal, chief Zibeon, chief Anah, chief Dishon, chief Ezer, chief Dishan. These are the chiefs descended from the Horites, according to their various chiefs in the land of Seir. Now these are the kings who reigned in the land of Edom before any king reigned over the sons of Israel. Bela the son of Beor reigned in Edom, and the name of his city was Dinhabah. Then Bela died, and Jobab the son of Zerah of Bozrah became king in his place. Then Jobab died, and Husham of the land of the Temanites

became king in his place. Then Husham died, and Hadad the son of Bedad, who defeated Midian in the field of Moab, became king in his place; and the name of his city was Avith. Then Hadad died, and Samlah of Masrekah became king in his place. Then Samlah died, and Shaul of Rehoboth on the Euphrates River became king in his place. Then Shaul died, and Baal-hanan the son of Achbor became king in his place. Then Baal-hanan the son of Achbor died, and Hadar became king in his place; and the name of his city was Pau; and his wife's name was Mehetabel, the daughter of Matred, daughter of Mezahab. Now these are the names of the chiefs descended from Esau, according to their families and their localities, by their names: chief Timna, chief Alvah, chief Jetheth, chief Oholibamah, chief Elah, chief Pinon, chief Kenaz, chief Teman, chief Mibzar, chief Magdiel, chief Iram. These are the chiefs of Edom (that is, Esau, the father of the Edomites), according to their habitations in the land of their possession" (36:20-43).

The Horites were the natives in the land of Edom, and they were living in the hill country of Seir to the southwest of the Dead Sea. They were once conquered by Chedorlaomer, king of Elam (Genesis 14:5-6), and later they were either destroyed or banished by the sons of Esau (Deuteronomy 2:12, 22).

These are the sons of Seir the Horite, the inhabitants of the land: Lotan and Shobal and Zibeon and Anah, and Dishon and Ezer and Dishan. These seven became the chiefs among the Horites in the land of Edom. The sons of Lotan were Hori and Hemam; and Lotan's sister was Timna. The sons of Shobal were Alvan and Manahath and Ebal, Shepho and Onam. The sons of Zibeon were Aiah and Anah.

Anah gave births to Dishon and Oholibamah. Dishon's sons were Hemdan and Eshban and Ithran and Cheran. The sons of Ezer were Bilhan and Zaavan and Akan. Dishan's sons were Uz and Aran. They were the chiefs descended from the Horites. Until they were conquered by the sons of Esau, they lived near the Dead Sea reigning over their respective areas.

After conquering the Horites and taking the hill country of Seir, the sons of Esau outnumbered the sons of Jacob. They had kings over them and they flourished. Before Israel, the sons of Jacob, had a king, Edom had already had kings over them.

From verse 31 onward, we read that the each of the eight sons of Esau became the kings of Edom in turn. First, Bela the son of Beor reigned in Edom. Then Bela died, and Jobab replaced him, and Jobab was replaced by Husham. Then Husham died, and Hadad the son of Bedad, who defeated Midian in the field of Moab, became king in his place. Then Hadad died, and Samlah became king in his place. Then Samlah died, and Shaul became king in his place. Then Baal-hanan, and then Hadar inherited the throne.

The chiefs from the sons of Esau can be categorized by their families and their localities. The first group was Timna, Alvah, Jetheth, Oholibamah, Elah, Pinon, Kenaz, Teman, Mibzar, Magdiel, and Iram. These were the chiefs of Edom and the names of their people were the names of the areas they were living in.

They had their respective reign in their independent localities in the hill country of Seir. But eventually, the Edomites that once thrived were driven out from the land when the sons of Israel were settling down in Canaan after the Exodus.

Jacob
Chapter 12

Joseph Sold As Slave into Egypt

Joseph Hated by His Brothers

Jacob Keeps Joseph's Dream in Mind

Joseph Goes to Find His Brothers in the Field

Brothers' Attempt on Joseph's Life

Joseph Sold into Egypt

The Sons Lie to Jacob

1. Joseph Hated by His Brothers

"Now Jacob lived in the land where his father had sojourned, in the land of Canaan. These are the records of the generations of Jacob. Joseph, when seventeen years of age, was pasturing the flock with his brothers while he was still a youth, along with the sons of Bilhah and the sons of Zilpah, his father's wives. And Joseph brought back a bad report about them to their father. Now Israel loved Joseph more than all his sons, because he was the son of his old age; and he made him a varicolored tunic. His brothers saw that their father loved him more than all his brothers; and so they hated him and could not speak to him on friendly terms" (Genesis 37:1-4).

God tried Jacob to build his character. Then He guided him to the land that He had promised to give and began to fulfill His plan through him. It was to establish God's elect Israel, and God knew that there needed to be a person who would play a crucial role in this process.

It was the person who would lay the foundations for Jacob and his sons to go into Egypt and form a great nation. God chose Joseph, the 11th son of Jacob. In the spiritual sense Joseph had the birthright. Also, he also had the most proper inner heart among the 12 sons.

Joseph was born in Haran. He moved to Canaan in his childhood. It is also where he lost his mother, Rachel. And he had now become 17 years old. He was wise and handsome in form. He had deep faith in God, too. He held the teachings of his father in mind and tried to keep them.

Jacob loved Joseph the most among his 12 sons. It was not only because he begot Joseph in his old age, but also because he was the first son of Rachel, his most beloved wife. He always put Joseph next to him and taught him. He loved him much more than other sons. He even made him a multicolored tunic unlike other sons.

Jacob did it because he loved Joseph, but it was this kind of an act that caused misfortune for him. As it is said, "they hated him and could not speak to him on friendly terms," Jacob's favoritism gave rise to jealousy in the brothers toward Joseph.

Jacob was changed through the trials, but he still had some remaining bias because he had not yet cultivated complete goodness. Of course, Jacob didn't think he was biased. But he did not consider everything with a broad view, and he was not able to realize or understand the hearts of other sons yet. This caused him to show favoritism. He lacked God's wisdom which comes from above (James 3:17-18).

Furthermore, Joseph made the situation worse by doing the things that could make his brothers hate him. He brought bad reports about his brothers to his father. They couldn't help but hate him. But it doesn't mean Joseph did it with evil intentions.

Although he was very young, he basically had a good heart, and his fundamental character was good, as well. He just thought it was the right thing to do when he was making the negative reports about his brothers to his father. It's just that he had his own righteousness. He loved his father and he wanted his brothers to do better.

But because he kind of got ahead of himself because of his self-righteousness, he wasn't able to think about covering the faults of his brothers. He formed a mental framework with the truth he had learned from his father, and this in turn gave hard times to his brothers. He thought he was doing the right thing, but in fact, he was making his brothers uncomfortable and alienating his brothers from his father.

This does not mean we have to cover somebody's fault all the time. If somebody is going the way of death, we should be able to guide them to the right way. If somebody is disgracing

God, we should be able to teach them the right thing for the sake of God's kingdom and the individual's soul.

What is important here is the attitude of heart. It is good to practice righteousness, but if we pass judgment on those who are not living a righteous life or if we reveal their fault immediately, it means we lack love and acceptance. When we reveal somebody's fault, our intention must not be just the disclosing of their fault itself; it has to be done with earnest love with which we want their souls to change.

If we have this kind of love, we will find a gentle way to let them understand their wrongdoings and touch their heart so that we can actually change them. But because Joseph was making the negative reports concerning his brothers from within the framework of his self-righteousness, it was impossible for his brothers to like him. They didn't like him in the first place due to their father's favoritism, and his actions only caused the situation to deteriorate.

2. Jacob Keeps Joseph's Dream in Mind

> *"Then Joseph had a dream, and when he told it to his brothers, they hated him even more. He said to them, 'Please listen to this dream which I have had; for behold, we were binding sheaves in the field, and lo, my sheaf rose up and also stood erect; and behold, your*

sheaves gathered around and bowed down to my sheaf.' Then his brothers said to him, 'Are you actually going to reign over us? Or are you really going to rule over us?' So they hated him even more for his dreams and for his words. Now he had still another dream, and related it to his brothers, and said, 'Lo, I have had still another dream; and behold, the sun and the moon and eleven stars were bowing down to me.' He related it to his father and to his brothers; and his father rebuked him and said to him, 'What is this dream that you have had? Shall I and your mother and your brothers actually come to bow ourselves down before you to the ground?' His brothers were jealous of him, but his father kept the saying in mind" (37:5-11).

In his imperfectness, Joseph had his self-righteousness, and along with this, he had the desire to reveal himself and to take all the love of his father, too. And such desires of his were clearly seen in the event where he related his dream to his brothers, as if he were bragging.

We can feel his lofty heart from the fact that he was telling his brothers in an imperative sentence to hear about his dream. His sentence contained pride about himself and his disregard concerning his brothers.

Since he had a very unusual dream, Joseph must have understood what it meant. He should have anticipated his brothers' reactions if he told them about it. But because his desire to brag about it prodded him on, he couldn't help but tell them about his dream.

The dream was that while Joseph and his brothers were binding sheaves in the field, Joseph's sheaf rose up and also stood erect; and his brothers' sheaves gathered around and bowed down to Joseph's sheaf.

The brothers couldn't take it happily. They replied, "Are you actually going to reign over us? Or are you really going to rule over us?" They hated him even more. Now, as the brother's reaction was not good, Joseph must have taken it into consideration and not talk about such a thing again. But without giving much thought about the situations or the heart of his brothers, Joseph talked about yet another dream.

This time, he said, "The sun and the moon and eleven stars were bowing down to me." One could easily understand that it meant not just his brothers but also his parents were bowing down before him. It agitated the brothers even more.

Joseph did not really pay attention to the response of his brothers; he went ahead and told his father about his dream, too. It means he wanted to bring his father to his side. Joseph had the desire to reveal himself and to be recognized by others.

But after hearing about the dream, Jacob rebuked Joseph saying, "What is this dream that you have had? Shall I and your mother and your brothers actually come to bow ourselves down before you to the ground?" Joseph thought his father was going to be on his side, but rather he only received a scolding from him.

What is the reason Jacob scolded Joseph? It's not because of the dream, but it was for Joseph's bragging attitude. Jacob also felt that that it was a bit too much.

Joseph could've quietly come to his father and talk about it, but he carelessly bragged about it before his brothers and caused them to hate him. Jacob wanted to point this out. Jacob also wanted to bring to his attention his boastful attitude and his disregard toward his brothers.

Yet, even as he reprimanded Joseph, Jacob kept the dream in his mind. Jacob hoped that Joseph's brothers' anger would cool down by his scolding Joseph.

But it was too late. Due to Jacob's favoritism that they had seen for a very long time, hatred toward Joseph had already been placed very deeply in the heart of the brothers. Their hard feelings only got worse after they heard about Joseph's dreams. Their feelings couldn't just go away by hearing their father rebuking Joseph this one time.

If Joseph's dream would come true, even Jacob had to bow before Joseph. But Jacob had no problem with that. It's because he loved him very much. If you love somebody, you are not jealous when they are well-off. But rather, you will only rejoice together.

But the brothers were different. Yes, they had hard feelings because of their father's favoritism, but at the same time they couldn't just accept the fact that their younger brother would be above them.

3. Joseph Goes to Find His Brothers in the Field

"Then his brothers went to pasture their father's flock in Shechem. Israel said to Joseph, 'Are not your brothers pasturing the flock in Shechem? Come, and I will send you to them.' And he said to him, 'I will go.' Then he said to him, 'Go now and see about the welfare of your brothers and the welfare of the flock, and bring word back to me.' So he sent him from the valley of Hebron, and he came to Shechem. A man found him, and behold, he was wandering in the field; and the man asked him, 'What are you looking for?' He said, 'I am looking for my brothers; please tell me where they are pasturing the flock.' Then the man said, 'They have moved from here; for I heard them say, "Let us go to Dothan."' So Joseph went after his brothers and found them at Dothan" (37:12-17).

We can see Jacob's favoritism toward Joseph once again. While Joseph's brothers were pasturing Jacob's flock in Shechem, Joseph stayed home. He was exempt from difficult and laborious work. His brothers couldn't stop having complaints against him.

In this situation, one day, Jacob told Joseph to go to his brothers and see about the welfare of his brothers and the welfare of the flock. Jacob had a reason. Of course it was to see how the sons were doing in the field, but he also wanted to comfort them while they were working so hard away from home. At the same time, he wanted to bring reconciliation between Joseph and his brothers, too.

Jacob also knew about the hard feelings that the other sons had toward Joseph. So, he thought those feelings might melt away if he sent Joseph on his behalf and comforted them. But Joseph's idea about this errand was a bit different.

Joseph became even prouder thinking that he had received some kind of special task from his father. He already had a boastful mindset and now he thought he had received a very special duty from his father, so he felt very good about himself.

Joseph set out to Shechem following the word of his father. But he couldn't find his brothers there. A shepherd always has to move from one place to another to find grass and water to pasture the flock.

Joseph was wandering around looking for his brothers, but fortunately, he met somebody who helped him. A man found him and asked him, "What are you looking for?" Joseph asked him where his brothers were pasturing the flock. It seems like they knew each other.

The man in the field did not ask Joseph what he was doing there but what he was looking for, as if he knew that Joseph was looking for something.

Joseph, too, just asked him where his brothers were, although he couldn't possibly be sure if the man knew the whereabouts of his brothers. And, as soon as Joseph asked him the man informed him that his brothers were in Dothan. It looks like everything had somehow been well-coordinated in advance.

What if Joseph hadn't met this man at that time? He probably would have wandered in the field for a while and then returned home without seeing his brothers. Consequently, he would not have been sold into slavery in Egypt nor would he have undergone the 13 years of trials in Egypt.

Of course, his trials could have been given through other events later. But in God's plan that moment was 'the moment'. Therefore, Joseph had to meet his brothers now. So, God did not just let Joseph go back home after wandering in the field. That is why He sent a man who could guide him to the place where his brothers were.

It was an angel sent by God. Of course, in Joseph's eyes he appeared in the form of a man. With His power, God can make angels appear as men. God sent His angel so Joseph could find his brothers. Only then could Joseph begin to receive his refining trials. This was the way to fulfill the providence of God.

Such a trial is a trial allowed by God Himself. After he received a great vision through his dream, he went through the refining trials, and as a result he got rid of self-righteousness, the disregard for others and his bragging. He also cultivated a deep level of goodness. God allowed the trials because He knew Joseph would be transformed through them. Thus, trials were a blessing for Joseph and a way of prosperity.

4. Brothers' Attempt on Joseph's Life

"When they saw him from a distance and before he came close to them, they plotted against him to put him to death. They said to one another, 'Here comes this dreamer! Now then, come and let us kill him and throw him into one of the pits; and we will say, "A wild beast devoured him." Then let us see what will become of his dreams!' But Reuben heard this and rescued him out of their hands and said, 'Let us not take his life.' Reuben further said to them, 'Shed no blood. Throw him into this pit that is in the wilderness, but do not lay hands on him' that he might rescue him out of their hands, to restore him to his father. So it came about, when Joseph reached his brothers, that they stripped Joseph of his tunic, the varicolored tunic that was on him; and they took him and threw him into the pit. Now the pit was empty, without any water in it" (37:18-24).

Finally, the incident began to take place as Joseph was arriving at Dothan where his brothers were. The brothers recognized him before he got close. They said to each other, "Here comes this dreamer! Now then, come and let us kill him and throw him into one of the pits; and we will say, 'A wild beast devoured him.' Then let us see what will become of his dreams!"

Through their conversation, we can see that they had the desire to harm Joseph for a long time. They just went ahead and made a plan to kill him without trying to find out why Joseph came to them. They agreed that they'd kill Joseph and throw the body into a pit and say that a wild animal killed him.

The brothers cynically referred to Joseph as 'dreamer' and this tells us the biggest reason they wanted to kill Joseph was his dreams. In other words, we can understand Joseph's dreams, in which the 11 brothers and the parents would bow down before him, hurt their feelings very much.

Of course, that didn't justify their plan to kill him. However, they just thought Joseph was getting what he deserved for his disrespect toward his older brothers and his father and for lifting himself up. And in this way of thinking they thought their actions were justified. Now there was no escape for Joseph.

At this moment, Reuben spoke up. He said not to take the boy's life. He said, "Shed no blood. Throw him into this pit that is in the wilderness, but do not lay hands on him." Reuben did not have good feelings toward Joseph either. So, what is the reason he tried to spare at least the life of Joseph?

Previously, Reuben committed adultery with his father's concubine, Bilhah. But Jacob did not reveal the fact or carry out the punishment. He just waited for them to repent and turn from their ways by themselves (Genesis 35:22). Reuben was well aware of this fact.

Since Reuben was shown great mercy by Jacob, he thought about the pain his father would have if Joseph had died. But at the same time, he knew he couldn't dissuade his brothers from harming Joseph either. For this reason he came up with an idea and suggested they not take the boy's life and just throw him into a pit.

And this sounded good in the ears of the brothers. Their goal would be achieved just by throwing him into a pit. They didn't have to kill him with their own hands because he would soon die in the pit. Some pits had water in it, and if you strip somebody and throw him into a pit, he couldn't last long because it was in the wilderness.

So, they stripped Joseph of his multicolored tunic and threw him into a pit. Fortunately, that pit did not have water in it. This was also God's intervention protecting Joseph's life. No life can be taken unless it is allowed by God who controls life and death.

5. Joseph Sold into Egypt

> "Then they sat down to eat a meal. And as they raised their eyes and looked, behold, a caravan of Ishmaelites was coming from Gilead, with their camels bearing aromatic gum and balm and myrrh, on their way to bring them down to Egypt. Judah said to his brothers, 'What profit is it for us to kill our brother and cover up his blood? Come and let us sell him to the Ishmaelites and not lay our hands on him, for he is our brother, our own flesh.' And his brothers listened to him. Then some Midianite traders passed by, so they pulled him up and lifted Joseph out of the pit, and sold him to the Ishmaelites for twenty shekels of silver. Thus they brought Joseph into Egypt" (37:25-28).

God knew exactly what kinds of refining trials Joseph had to go through before he could become the prime minister of Egypt. For that reason God let each event take place step by step.

When Joseph came all the way to Dothan to find them, the brothers threw him into a pit. Then, while they were eating together, they saw the caravan of Ishmaelites who were going down to Egypt. God let the Ishmaelites pass by that place at that exact moment.

They were taking aromatic gum and balm and myrrh to Egypt on their camels. They were expensive goods. It tells us they were merchants with some class. That is why they could sell Joseph to the captain of the royal guard of Egypt.

Joseph was sold not as an ordinary servant, but into the house of the captain of the bodyguard. This was the first step for Joseph to become the prime minister of Egypt later. On the outside he was sold as a mere slave, but it was actually a steppingstone for him to become the prime minister. Each of these things was fulfilled without an error in the providence of God.

Here, the one who played the decisive role in selling Joseph to the Ishmaelites was Judah. Judah said it would be of no use if they killed their own brother and hid the fact, and he suggested they sell him to the merchants and not lay their hands on him. He reminded the brothers Joseph was their own brother and blood. The brothers listened to Judah and Joseph's life was spared. The Ishmaelites bought Joseph for 20 pieces of silver and brought him to Egypt.

For Israel that was formed through the 12 sons of Jacob to become a nation, they needed to be protected within the safety of Egypt's borders. And, to fulfill this plan of God, Joseph was used as God's instrument. However, his brothers were used as bad instruments in the process of Joseph going to Egypt. Reuben and Judah were used as somewhat less evil instruments because they at least spared Joseph's life.

It is not that God designates certain persons to be used as

good instruments and others as evil ones. God knows the heart and vessel of each one, and He uses them accordingly. It is each person that makes his own decisions. Namely, we are used by God for different purposes depending on the good or evil choices that we make.

6. The Sons Lie to Jacob

> "Now Reuben returned to the pit, and behold, Joseph was not in the pit; so he tore his garments. He returned to his brothers and said, 'The boy is not there; as for me, where am I to go?' So they took Joseph's tunic, and slaughtered a male goat and dipped the tunic in the blood; and they sent the varicolored tunic and brought it to their father and said, 'We found this; please examine it to see whether it is your son's tunic or not.' Then he examined it and said, 'It is my son's tunic. A wild beast has devoured him; Joseph has surely been torn to pieces!' So Jacob tore his clothes, and put sackcloth on his loins and mourned for his son many days. Then all his sons and all his daughters arose to comfort him, but he refused to be comforted. And he said, 'Surely I will go down to Sheol in mourning for my son.' So his father wept for him. Meanwhile, the Midianites sold him in Egypt to Potiphar, Pharaoh's officer, the captain of the bodyguard" (37:29-36).

Reuben was not present when Judah persuaded the brothers to sell Joseph to the Ishmaelites. When he returned and found that Joseph was gone, how shocked he must have been!

He tore his garments in torment. He didn't know what to do to resolve the situation. He tried to save Joseph but he was gone. The situation had already gone to an irreversible state.

Now they had only two choices. They could come clean with their father about what they had done, or they had to lie to him. They chose to lie. They slaughtered a male goat and dipped Joseph's tunic in its blood. And they brought the tunic to their father and asked him to see if it was Joseph's. They piled sin upon sin by cheating their father in addition to selling their brother as a slave.

Jacob immediately recognized that the varicolored tunic was Joseph's. He was so shocked he tore his clothes and put sackcloth on his loins and mourned for his son many days.

If Jacob had exerted a little bit of self-control over his emotions and thought about the situation, he wouldn't have been deceived so easily. It'd been very difficult for all 10 sons to get their stories straight, so if he asked them about the situation more calmly, he'd have realized their lie.

But he was engulfed by his sorrow thinking he lost Joseph, and he couldn't assess the situation with reason. Just by seeing Joseph's bloodstained tunic he thought Joseph had died, and he fell into despair and sorrow. He even refused to be comforted by his other children.

And seeing their father show favoritism even at this moment, the sons felt they had done well rather than having pangs of conscience for their crime.

Also, Jacob said something he must have never said as a person who believed in God, even though we consider the fact that the sorrow of losing Joseph was great. It is that he said, "Surely I will go down to Sheol in mourning for my son." It means he wanted to die, too.

Of course, his grief must have been unbearable after losing Joseph whom he loved so much on top of losing her beloved wife Rachel. And yet, spiritually speaking his words were the words of unbelief.

The dream and vision God gave to Jacob were truly amazing and great. Jacob had the duty to lay the foundation of the nation of Israel. But just because one of his sons died he wanted to follow him to death, and it was not right in the sight of God at all.

Jacob went through a great deal of change in character after he demolished his ego at Jabbok River, but when this unbearable situation struck him, his lack of faith was revealed. It was in great contrast with the faith of his grandfather Abraham.

Abraham had always drawn a clear line between God's work and his personal matters, and his priority was always God. He begot Ishmael through Sarah's maid Hagar, before he begot Isaac.

And Abraham loved both Ishmael and Isaac without any discrimination. But when he understood that Ishmael had to leave Isaac for the providence of God to be fulfilled, he immediately sent Hagar and Ishmael away. He didn't cling to fleshly affection but strictly followed the will of God.

When God commanded him to give Isaac as a burnt offering, Abraham did not hold on to any fleshly affection or personal feelings. It's not because he did not love his family. He was full of love, more than anybody else, but his love did not have any part of the matter when he was carrying out God's will. It's because he did away with fleshly affection and desires completely (Galatians 5:24).

In doing God's work, there should be absolutely no ulterior motives or fleshly emotions. Those who have faith and who love God will consider brothers and sisters of faith first, rather than their own family members or those who are close to them.

But that does not mean you can neglect your family. It just means that you should not love your family in a fleshly sense that puts your family above the things of God.

Nowhere in the Bible did Abraham want to give up his

duties just because the burden was heavy. God once said to him, *"And I will make you a great nation, and I will bless you, and make your name great; and so you shall be a blessing"* (Genesis 12:2). This was his duty as much as it was a covenant given by God.

And Abraham knew there were some things that he had to carry out to fulfill this duty. In a fleshly way of thinking it was such a great burden. Had he not had such a duty, he didn't have to send Ishmael away. He didn't have to go through the test of offering Isaac as a burnt offering. He didn't have to send away his six sons he begot from his second wife Keturah. He could have spent his last days with so many children with happiness and satisfaction.

But he gave up all these things in order to complete his duty and the providence of God that would be fulfilled through Isaac. Compared to Abraham, Jacob's words and actions were still very immature. He put his sorrow and personal feelings ahead of his God-given duty and God's works.

Meanwhile, Getting back to Joseph, the Midianites sold him in Egypt to Potiphar, Pharaoh's officer, the captain of the bodyguard. Joseph, who used to be loved by his father so much, suddenly became a slave in a foreign country overnight. So, did he fall into despair? He didn't.

From his heart Joseph believed in the dream given by God, and he did not waver at all in all those years of trials. It seemed like the situations were getting worse, but such things could not shake Joseph's faith.

Jacob

Chapter 13

Judah and Perez, Orthodox Family of Abraham

Faith of Judah the Fourth Son of Jacob

Curses on Judah's Children

Judah and Tamar His Daughter-In-Law

Judah's Sons Perez and Zerah

1. Faith of Judah the Fourth Son of Jacob

"And it came about at that time that Judah departed from his brothers and visited a certain Adullamite, whose name was Hirah. Judah saw there a daughter of a certain Canaanite whose name was Shua; and he took her and went in to her. So she conceived and bore a son and he named him Er. Then she conceived again and bore a son and named him Onan. She bore still another son and named him Shelah; and it was at Chezib that she bore him" (38:1-5).

In the middle of explaining about Joseph, the Bible suddenly talks about Judah in Genesis chapter 38. Here lies an important spiritual meaning.

Joseph's having been sold into Egypt was the key for Israel to become large in number and to grow up as the elect of God. It was also the beginning point for the sons of Israel to be enslaved in Egypt for 400 years and then become a big nation.

Israel's slavery in Egypt, the Exodus from Egypt, and going back to the Promised Land of Canaan all serve as symbolism for the ministry of salvation of Jesus the Messiah.

It is the same with our process of going into heavenly kingdom: we were slaves of the enemy devil and Satan, but we received forgiveness of sins and were set free from darkness through Jesus Christ. Then we can receive the heavenly kingdom by walking in the Light, that is, in the Word of God.

Joseph's having been sold into Egypt was the beginning of his trials on a personal level, but in a spiritually broader sense, it was the beginning of the providence of God that was to be fulfilled.

At this point, God suddenly mentions Judah and his children. The content in Genesis chapter 38 is not just some unhappy history of an individual. It gives us a glimpse about Jesus who would come as the Messiah.

Revelation 5:5 says, *"...and one of the elders said to me, 'Stop weeping; behold, the Lion that is from the tribe of Judah, the Root of David, has overcome so as to open the book and its seven seals.'"*

Micah 5:2 also says, *"But as for you, Bethlehem Ephrathah, too little to be among the clans of Judah, from you One will go forth for Me to be ruler in Israel. His goings forth are from long ago, from the days of eternity."*

Of course, Jesus can't have any physical genealogy for He was conceived by the Holy Spirit. But He needed a physical genealogy in a sense that He had to put on a human body. Jesus was born among the tribe of Judah according to the prophecy in the Old Testament and it further confirmed He is the Messiah who was prophesied.

Jacob's sons heard about God from their father. They heard about the faithful God who fulfills His promises and who compensates our actions. Although they received the same teaching, the heart and faith of each of his sons were different from one another.

Amidst trials Joseph always revered God and believed in the faithful God. He did not commit sins before God in any situation. He never lost the dream given by God. But his brothers were different. We can see what kind of faith they had from Genesis chapter 38. It appears to be about Judah, but it also tells us about the faith of other brothers.

Judah heard and learned about God, but he didn't really believe in God completely from his heart. He offered sacrifices from time to time but it was only formality. He just served God the way he saw fit without casting away evil from his heart. That is why he took as his wife a daughter of a certain Canaanite whose name was Shua.

Judah certainly knew what his father Jacob and his

grandfather Abraham did to get a wife. And yet, he took a Gentile woman, and it tells us he didn't have enough faith to practice the word of God. He just did what he liked. So, what kinds of faith would Judah's children have, considering that they were born of a gentile woman? They'd have fallen into gentile customs and sins, and it must have been difficult for them even to keep their faith in God.

God strictly prohibited intermarrying with Gentiles. It's because they could've been affected. They could've accepted the wrong customs and evil deeds of the gentile races. Especially, although marrying is a very important event of a lifetime, Judah didn't even consult his father Jacob at all. If he had consulted his father and not married a gentile woman, the tragedies in the family wouldn't have taken place.

Of course, just because Judah didn't consult Jacob, it doesn't mean he didn't learn the will of God. Though he knew the will of God, He just took a gentile woman as a wife because he wanted to. This is the difference between just knowing the word of God, and believing it in the heart. Even though we know the word of truth, we will forsake it following our benefit and lusts, as long as we do not cast away evil from our heart. We will just take the way that seems good to us the way Judah did.

2. Curses on Judah's Children

"Now Judah took a wife for Er his firstborn, and her name was Tamar. But Er, Judah's firstborn, was evil in the sight of the LORD, so the LORD took his life. Then Judah said to Onan, 'Go in to your brother's wife, and perform your duty as a brother-in-law to her, and raise up offspring for your brother.' Onan knew that the offspring would not be his; so when he went in to his brother's wife, he wasted his seed on the ground in order not to give offspring to his brother. But what he did was displeasing in the sight of the LORD; so He took his life also. Then Judah said to his daughter-in-law Tamar, 'Remain a widow in your father's house until my son Shelah grows up'; for he thought, 'I am afraid that he too may die like his brothers.' So Tamar went and lived in her father's house" (38:6-11).

Judah married a Canaanite woman against God's will, and begot three sons: Er, Onan, and Shelah. Time passed, and when Er was getting a wife, Judah still did what he liked to do.

Abraham committed all the matters to God when he was getting a wife for his son, Isaac. In order to get the daughter-in-law from his own people and not among the Gentiles, he sent his most trusted servant to Haran. By the grace of God, the servant met Rebekah, the granddaughter of Nahor who was Abraham's brother.

But Judah at his discretion got a woman as his daughter-in-law. He just decided pretty much everything in the household as he saw fit. His first son Er took a Canaanite woman as his wife, and unfortunately he died young without leaving any children behind. He was evil as it is said, "But Er, Judah's firstborn, was evil in the sight of the LORD, so the LORD took his life."

But we should not misunderstand this verse and say God actually kills people. This event of God taking Er's life is similar to Ananias and Sapphira's case; they lied to Peter, which was in effect trying to cheat the Holy Spirit, and thus they were cursed, and they fell and died immediately.

In this case, some might think the punishment was too harsh for their sin. But it is not that they fell and died just because they lied to a man of God once. It is actually the curse of God fell upon them because of the sins they had been storing up for a long time.

But this was a special case anyway. For the most people, if their sins are accumulated and it goes over a certain limit, God cannot protect them from disasters or accidents that might come upon them according to justice. So, Er was cursed and died because of so much evil that he had been piling up before God.

As Judah's first son Er did not leave any children, his younger brother Onan took his sister-in-law Tamar. It was a marriage to succeed the generation. If the first son dies without a child, the second son would take his brother's wife.

It was a custom to continue the genealogy of the family when the first son died without a child.

The brothers of the dead had to fulfill this duty with mercy, sacrifice, and the brotherly love. But Onan, who had the duty to continue the family line for Er, refused to do this duty. Knowing that his child that would be born through his brother's wife couldn't be his own, he wasted the seeds on the ground not to let his sister-in-law become pregnant.

It was evil in the sight of God and God took away his life as well. One might wonder if Onan's act was that evil, but when God said Onan was evil, it was not only about this isolated single incident.

The Bible says Onan did so in order not to give offspring to his brother. If his brother's wife gave birth to a son, the birthright of the family would go to him, and Onan didn't want that to happen.

If there was no son from his older brother, he could have the birthright, and he thought it was a waste to let his sister-in-law have a son and hand over the birthright to him. He didn't have any mercy or sense of sacrifice for his brother. He had only greed desiring to take the birthright.

Especially at that time, people considered it great curse for the genealogy of a family to be severed. Therefore, Onan's act was to ignore his whole family falling into a curse. We can see how evil his heart was just from this incident.

Onan had been storing up a lot of evil before God, and eventually he forsook his duty to his dead brother, and he had to pay for his evil with death.

And in the process of Onan going into Tamar, Judah insisted on his own ideas. When Er died, he did not ask Onan his opinion or try to persuade him from fulfilling his brotherly duty. All that Judah thought about was the family line had to continue regardless of Onan's opinion.

In fact, such an act stemmed from the victim mentality and his strong attachments to birthright that he acquired during his growth. His father, Jacob, had shown extreme favoritism toward Joseph and even tried to hand over the birthright to him, and Judah deeply held grudges against it. Such mindset came out as the action to oppress or force Onan to fulfill family duty.

This was one of the reasons why Onan didn't want to obey his father. Along with the rebellious mind, he just followed his greed and evil. He went into his sister-in-law because he was forced by his father, but he came up with a way to prevent pregnancy.

Anyway, after losing two sons, Judah wanted his third son Shelah to continue the blood line, but he couldn't help his hesitation. He was worried that the main cause for death of his two sons could have been his daughter-in-law Tamar. He was worried his third son might also die because of her.

So, Judah sent Tamar away to her own household saying Shelah was too young. He said he'd call her again after Shelah grew up, but he didn't want to give Shelah to her at all.

What would Judah have done if he were a true man of God? When things were going wrong in his household, he'd have prayed to God or at least consult his father Jacob to understand God's will. But he just dealt with the situations on hand as he seemed fit. He just wanted to send his daughter-in-law away without considering her situation at all.

If he didn't want to give his third son to her, he should've given her freedom so she could remarry. But he just sent Tamar back to her own family by telling her a lie. Then even after his third son grew up, he didn't contact her again. He just forgot about Tamar who was living a lonely life without a single child.

But in the Bible, we can see a person who acted in a very different way than that of Judah in a very similar situation. It was Naomi, the mother-in-law of Ruth. Naomi lost her husband and two grown-up sons in the land of Moab. Only Naomi herself and two daughters-in-law remained of the family.

One day, she decided to go back to her home country Israel and urged the two daughters-in-law to go back to their own families. She gave them freedom to remarry and seek a happier life without being bound by their duty to their mother-in-law, for their husbands had died and they had no hope of having children.

If Naomi thought about her standpoint only, it would've been very difficult to make such a decision. It'd have been much better for her to spend her last years of life with her two daughters-in-law than being alone. But she thought about her daughters-in-law who still had future rather than her own comfort.

Hearing the words of her mother-in-law, Orpah went back to her own family while weeping. But Ruth did not leave Naomi. She came to Israel and served her with love. Unlike this Naomi who thought about her daughters-in-law first, Judah only thought about his own viewpoint.

3. Judah and Tamar His Daughter-In-Law

"Now after a considerable time Shua's daughter, the wife of Judah, died; and when the time of mourning was ended, Judah went up to his sheepshearers at Timnah, he and his friend Hirah the Adullamite. It was told to Tamar, 'Behold, your father-in-law is going up to Timnah to shear his sheep.' So she removed her widow's garments and covered herself with a veil, and wrapped herself, and sat in the gateway of Enaim, which is on the road to Timnah; for she

saw that Shelah had grown up, and she had not been given to him as a wife. When Judah saw her, he thought she was a harlot, for she had covered her face. So he turned aside to her by the road, and said, 'Here now, let me come in to you'; for he did not know that she was his daughter-in-law. And she said, 'What will you give me, that you may come in to me?' He said, therefore, 'I will send you a young goat from the flock.' She said, moreover, 'Will you give a pledge until you send it?' He said, 'What pledge shall I give you?' And she said, 'Your seal and your cord, and your staff that is in your hand.' So he gave them to her and went in to her, and she conceived by him. Then she arose and departed, and removed her veil and put on her widow's garments" (Genesis 38:12-19).

Shelah grew up but Judah did not tell Tamar anything, and Tamar felt she was lied to and cheated. She resented all the years during which she waited only for Shelah believing her father-in-law Judah's words.

But she wouldn't just back away. As soon as she realized waiting wouldn't solve any problem, she devised a meticulous way. She planned to continue the bloodline by cheating her father-in-law Judah.

We can see that she is also seeking her own within her fleshly thoughts. She could say she didn't have a choice in order to continue the genealogy of the family, but in fact inwardly she had hard-feelings against her father-in-law and the desire to keep her rights. Tamar had been enduring until now hoping to recover the rights as the first daughter-in-law of the family, and she couldn't just give it up now. She refused giving up her desire to continue the genealogy.

So, she did something that could look very shameful in a physical sense. One day, she made herself look like a prostitute, and approached and seduced her father-in-law Judah who came to Timnah to his sheepshearers. As she planned, she conceived a child.

Tamar had wisdom of her own, and her plans were very detailed. She knew her action could cause misunderstanding of the people, so she made a plan to deal with that problem, too. When she was seducing her father-in-law Judah, she got the seal and his cord, and his staff that was in his hand as a pledge, so that Judah couldn't deny his action later.

4. Judah's Sons Perez and Zerah

"When Judah sent the young goat by his friend the Adullamite, to receive the pledge from the woman's hand, he did not find her. He asked the men of her place, saying, 'Where is the temple prostitute who was by the road at Enaim?' But they said, 'There has been no temple prostitute here.' So he returned to Judah, and said, 'I did not find her; and furthermore, the men of the place said, "There has been

no temple prostitute here."' Then Judah said, 'Let her keep them, otherwise we will become a laughingstock. After all, I sent this young goat, but you did not find her.' Now it was about three months later that Judah was informed, 'Your daughter-in-law Tamar has played the harlot, and behold, she is also with child by harlotry.' Then Judah said, 'Bring her out and let her be burned!' It was while she was being brought out that she sent to her father-in-law, saying, 'I am with child by the man to whom these things belong.' And she said, 'Please examine and see, whose signet ring and cords and staff are these?' Judah recognized them, and said, 'She is more righteous than I, inasmuch as I did not give her to my son Shelah.' And he did not have relations with her again. It came about at the time she was giving birth, that behold, there were twins in her womb. Moreover, it took place while she was giving birth, one put out a hand, and the midwife took and tied a scarlet thread on his hand, saying, 'This one came out first.' But it came about as he drew back his hand, that behold, his brother came out. Then she said, 'What a breach you have made for yourself!' So he was named Perez. Afterward his brother came out who had the scarlet thread on his hand; and he was named Zerah" (38:20-30).

Soon after that Judah sent a young goat through his friend to the prostitute to get his seal, cord and staff back from her. But the woman was nowhere to be found. Especially, they were surprised to hear there was no prostitute around that place.

Judah gave up looking for her in fear that they might become a laughingstock.

About 3 months later, Judah heard that Tamar his daughter-in-law became pregnant. He said to the people to bring her out and burn her. Tamar was accused of playing harlotry. Then, Tamar sent a person to show the seal, cord, and staff which belonged to the man who got her pregnant.

Judah now realized what really happened and said, "She is more righteous than I, inasmuch as I did not give her to my son Shelah." He admitted his fault. Such an event wouldn't have taken place had he given Shelah his son to Tamar. His lies caused such an incident.

Finally, Tamar gave birth to a twin. Their names were Perez and Zerah. The bloodline of Judah continued through Perez. In this way, the names Tamar and her son Perez went on in the genealogy of Jesus who came by the tribe of Judah (Matthew 1:3).

Then, why did God choose Judah as the orthodox bloodline of Jacob and let Jesus be born of that tribe? Why didn't God choose Joseph, who was the supposed to be the first son in spiritual sense and who had the best inner heart?

Each of the brothers and sisters has a different heart, mind, and vessel even though they have the same parents. Some are good, others are evil, and still others cause the wrath of God and become cursed. Even though the parents are good, the children might inherit evil traits from ancestors and even though the parents are evil, the children might inherit good traits from the ancestors.

Also, they all come to have different characters depending on how they form their 'self'. God knows about everything as good and evil crisscross and coexist, and for each moment in time, He chose relatively good and proper individuals in His heart to continue the genealogy of Jesus.

Of course Joseph had the best inner heart among the 12 sons of Jacob. But he already had the biggest duty which nobody could fulfill. It was to become the prime minister of Egypt and prepare the way for the sons of Israel to form a big nation. This duty could be fulfilled only through Joseph who had good enough heart and big enough vessel to do it.

So, God let Judah continue the family line of Jesus. Compared to Abraham, Isaac, and Jacob, Judah lacked a lot to be able to continue the orthodox genealogy, but he had the best mindset among the 12 sons of Jacob except for Joseph. When the brothers planned to kill Joseph, Judah advised they do not take Joseph's life, and Joseph's life was spared.

Also, when his fault was revealed by Tamar's incident, he did not try to hide it or just dodge the bullet but honestly accepted it was his fault. In Genesis chapter 44, when Benjamin was accused of being a thief and got into a situation where he could become a slave in Egypt, Judah said he would take the punishment on Benjamin's behalf. We cannot say Judah's heart was excellent and he had some evil, too, but he had the willingness to pursue the right way.

Jesus did not inherit any physical attributes from any man in His genealogy because He was conceived by the Holy Spirit. Thus, His genealogy can be considered as formality. And yet, God chose those who had relatively good hearts to be in the genealogy.

We've considered the difference between the acts of Judah and Naomi, and we can see Tamar was also very different from Ruth with regard to goodness. One might argue the action of Tamar and that of Ruth were different because the ways they were treated by Judah and Naomi respectively were very different. But it was rather they had fundamentally different heart than the way they were treated that they showed different actions.

Following her mother-in-law Naomi, Ruth went to a land foreign to her, to Israel. There, she completely sacrificed and dedicated herself to serve her mother-in-law. In the process of remarrying Boaz according to the law of the redemption of the land in Israel, she did not try to serve her own interest at all. She just followed her mother-in-law Naomi's will.

She did not think about her own comfort or benefit. She

completely followed her mother-in-law's will to continue the family. Because she had such good heart, God caused all things to work together for good, and her name could go on the genealogy of Jesus despite the fact that she was a Gentile woman. Her good deeds are recorded in one whole book among the 66 books of the Bible, and she went into a very glorious and precious position in the kingdom of heaven, too.

But it was not the same with Tamar. Perhaps one might argue that her undesirable plans came from her sense of duty to continue the family and from the fact her father-in-law had lied to her. It does not mean, however, her actions could be justified. If she had a better heart, she could have sought better ways to continue the bloodline.

Probably she could've moved the heart of Judah so he would want to give Shelah to her. But Tamar utilized fleshly wisdom and not spiritual wisdom. Of course, Tamar did continue the family line of Judah and her name is written in Jesus' genealogy, but her actions cannot give her any rewards in Heaven.

Why then did God allow this incident of Tamar to take place knowing Jesus would come from the tribe of Judah? Certainly, God could've prevented this shameful event from happening in the first place.

However, this incident contains the meaning that anyone who comes to Jesus Christ can be forgiven of their sins and be saved, whether they are good or evil. Jesus came to this earth not just to save the good people but also the evil and filthy ones, too, just as He said in Mark 2:17, *"It is not those who are healthy who need a physician, but those who are sick; I did not come to call the righteous, but sinners."*

Also, God does not only choose those who are good from the beginning to fulfill His providence. In the providence of God are various kinds of vessels, vessels that are made of gold, silver, or clay; and not all vessels are clean from the beginning, either. One can be used by God for noble purposes to the extent that they cleanse themselves with water to become purified in the Lord.

Therefore, considering the fact that Jesus was born of the tribe of Judah, one cannot say, "I was born of unfavorable parents and had unfavorable circumstances so how can I be used by God?" Anybody can become precious instruments that are used in the providence of God as long as they realize themselves through the Word of God and change themselves through prayers.

Jacob's Confession Reminiscing over His Past

Through the long-time trials, Jacob understood the justice and love of God. He learned about good and evil and before his death; he offered up confessions of thanksgiving before God who has established him as the father of Israel.

When I was truly foolish,
I had willingness to go against the will of the Father,
I had my own will to do the things my own way,
And I wanted to achieve with my own wisdom.
But I have realized that all those things were nothing.

My God,
As I met God and as I learned about God in my heart
In the ways of trials,
I hope all those who have come by me
Will keep the heart of God in their minds,
And remember it,
So that they will fulfill the works of God.

Although there were explosive things,
Hardships, and difficulties
While living my life as given here,
The grace and blessings
That You have given me, Father,
Are so great, how can I give You thanks enough!

Truly, my God,
And God of my father, and God of my grandfather,
My beloved God, I give You thanks
For changing me to be who I am now
And to be with You.

Now, accept me.
And, my God, let me be where You are
So that my heart will be in peaceful comfort.
I believe that You will fulfill
Your will and providence in me,
And that You will achieve what You have promised
Through the ones that remain.

I give You thanks,
That You loved me and let me be in Your grace.
I give thanks before God,
That now all the tears, pain of the heart, sorrow,
Parting with my beloved one,
And all other things buried in my heart
Come as perfect comfort in my heart in God.

I give thanks,
That through all these things that happened to me
Even at this moment as I am closing my eyes
You let me see and accomplish all things in Your providence.

The Twelve Tribes of Israel in Revelation

> *"...the tribe of Judah, twelve thousand were sealed, from the tribe of Reuben twelve thousand, from the tribe of Gad twelve thousand, the tribe of Asher twelve thousand, from the tribe of Naphtali twelve thousand, from the tribe of Manasseh twelve thousand, the tribe of Simeon twelve thousand, from the tribe of Levi twelve thousand, from the tribe of Issachar twelve thousand, the tribe of Zebulun twelve thousand, from the tribe of Joseph twelve thousand, from the tribe of Benjamin, twelve thousand were sealed" (Revelation 7:5-8).*

The 12 sons of Jacob were: Reuben, Simeon, Levi, Judah, Dan, Naphtali, Gad, Asher, Issachar, Zebulun, Joseph, and Benjamin. They were born in this order. They became the pillars to form the nation of Israel, continuing the family of Jacob, their father, who wrestled and overcame God at Jabbok.

Levi was excluded because they became the priests, and the two sons of Joseph Manasseh and Ephraim replaced Levi, so in total Israel became 12 tribes. It was done in the providence of God. God already moved the heart of Jacob in Egypt to bless Ephraim and Manasseh. Genesis 48:5 says, *"Now your two sons, who were born to you in the land of Egypt before I came to you in Egypt, are mine; Ephraim and Manasseh shall be*

mine, as Reuben and Simeon are." Later, each of them became one of the 12 tribes and received the land in Canaan.

However, we see that in the book of Revelation chapter 7 the 12 tribes are a little different from those of Genesis. They are: Judah, Reuben, Gad, Asher, Naphtali, Manasseh, Simeon, Levi, Issachar, Zebulun, Joseph, and Benjamin. Dan was excluded from the original 12 sons of Jacob, and Manasseh replaced him. It's because Dan took the lead in idolatry (1 Kings 12:28-29).

The order of the 12 tribes of Israel written in Revelation chapter 7 is different from the order of birth of Jacob's son. This is not because the order in Revelation was written at random but because it was written according to the spiritual meaning contained in each of their names.

We can achieve complete holiness if we understand the meaning contained in the names of the 12 tribes and cultivate them. In order to explain these levels of holiness, the names of the 12 tribes in Revelation were written according to the spiritual meanings and not according to the order of birth.

The Spiritual Meaning of Number '12' in the Bible

In many cases the numbers in the Bible carry spiritual

meanings.

For example, number '3' is number of 'being right' or 'being proper', which means it accomplishes perfection. God exists as the Triune God – the Father, the Son, and the Holy Spirit. Jesus resurrected on the third day after the crucifixion. Jonah was in the belly of the big fish for 3 days. Jesus was tested 3 times before He began His ministry.

Number '4' is number of 'suffering'. The sons of Israel went through trials in the wilderness for 40 years. Abraham's descendants went to Egypt and returned to Canaan after 4 generations. Jesus fasted for 40 days before He began His public ministry.

Number '7' is 'perfect number' which symbolizes perfection. God created all things for 6 days and rested on the 7th day. Naaman washed himself in the Jordan River 7 times before he was healed of leprosy. Elijah prayed 7 times to receive rain after a long drought.

Number '17' contains the meaning that God Himself governs and acts. The beginning date of Noah's flood is 17th day of the 2nd month. After the water withdrew, Noah's ark landed on Mt. Ararat on the 17th day of the 7th month. This symbolizes that God Himself governed the judgment of flood at the time of Noah. As for Joseph, he was sold into Egypt at the age of 17. This was the beginning point of the providence of God through him.

Number '12' is the number of light. Jesus said in John 11:9, "Are there not twelve hours in the day? If anyone walks in the day, he does not stumble, because he sees the light of this world." In the Bible the number of light '12' appears often. There are 12 tribes of Israel, 12 disciples of Jesus, 12 foundations of the city of New Jerusalem, 12 Pearl Gates, and the 12 fruits of the tree of life.

Number '12' appears usually when explaining about important providence of God. It is spiritually a very important number. The Lord Jesus is the true and perfect light that is the brightest like the light of the noon. He came down to this earth in human body to fulfill the providence of human salvation. Jesus was born in Israel, which is a nation formed by the 12 sons of Jacob. Jesus had 12 disciples to stand for the fact that Jesus Christ who is the true light will be preached.

144,000 Preachers and Gleaning Salvation

Once the gospel is preached to the ends of the earth, the Lord will come again as the King of kings and the Lord of lords. Those who are saved will be transformed to have the resurrected body; and they will be caught up into the air and participate in the 7-Year Wedding Banquet. On the other hand, those who are remaining on this earth will experience the 7-Year Great Tribulation.

There will be some individuals who will preach the gospel of Jesus Christ during the 7-Year Tribulation. 12,000 from each tribe of the 12 tribes of Israel will be chosen as these individuals. The 12 tribes of Israel do not only have the literal meaning. In spiritual sense, it refers to those who are chosen by God. There will be a large number of people, 144,000, because there will be only a short time, 7 years, to preach the gospel.

They receive this special duty during the 7-Year Tribulation and save many souls. There will be despair because the Holy Spirit will have been taken away and it will seem that there is no more hope of salvation. And they will preach the way of salvation once again, thereby accomplishing 'gleaning salvation'. Just as farmers glean the field after the harvest, the official human cultivation will have been over already, but God gives the souls one more chance of salvation.

The 144,000 preachers will preach to those who have never heard the gospel. They will accept Jesus Christ as their personal Savior and will receive salvation. Most of them will die in natural disasters or in the wars. It is relatively much easier death than being tortured to death.

Contrary to those who die relatively easier death, there will be people who will not be saved unless they are martyred. They are those who had already heard the gospel and even accepted the Lord and confessed their faith before the Second Coming of the Lord. But because they didn't have true faith, they remained as 'chaff' believers, and thus they won't be caught up in the air.

For these people, they can be saved only when they keep their faith by not receiving the mark of the beast amidst the inexpressible tortures. But the tortures will be so cruel that only a few will overcome and be saved. Therefore, no one who has already heard the gospel should fall into the 7-Year Tribulation for not having true faith.

God of love gave His only begotten Son Jesus on the Cross as the propitiation, thereby opening the way of salvation for everyone who believes. In the end time when the Lord's Second Coming is very near, God will pour out the Holy Spirit and work with the explosions of His power so that as many souls as possible can have faith.

2 Peter 3:8-9 says, *"But do not let this one fact escape your notice, beloved, that with the Lord one day is like a thousand years, and a thousand years like one day. The Lord is not slow about His promise, as some count slowness, but is patient toward you, not wishing for any to perish but for all to come to repentance."* As said, I hope all the readers will understand the deep and vast love of God who wants to give the opportunity of salvation to as many souls as possible and reach salvation.

The Names of the Twelve Tribes on the Twelve Gates of New Jerusalem

"...having the glory of God. Her brilliance was like a very costly stone, as a stone of crystal-clear jasper. It had a great and high wall, with twelve gates, and at the gates twelve angels; and names were written on them, which are the names of the twelve tribes of the sons of Israel" **(Revelation 21:11-12).**

Revelation chapter 21 writes about the city of New Jerusalem, which is as clear and beautiful as crystal and has the glory of God. It's a cube with its length, width, and height 1,500 miles each. There are 12 Pearl Gates on the wall, and the roads inside the city are made with gold. And what is the reason why the names of the 12 tribes of Israel are written on the 12 Pearl Gates?

After Adam and Eve were driven out from the Garden of Eden to this earth, they gave birth to a lot of children. The world became rapidly evil, and it was so full of sins and evil that God lamented over creating human beings. 1,600 years after the Fall, everyone had to be punished by the flood except for Noah and his family. And 400 years after that, Abraham was born. It was about 4,000 years ago.

God refined and established Abraham as the Father of Faith and promised him that his descendants would be as many as the stars in the sky (Genesis 22:17-18). Jacob was born in Abraham's bloodline; and Jacob begot 12 sons; and through these 12 sons the 12 tribes of Israel were formed.

God laid the foundation to form a nation through these 12 tribes. He also sent Jesus through the tribe of Judah to open the way of salvation for all peoples. And it is to symbolize this fact that He engraved the names of the 12 tribes of Israel on the 12 Pearl Gates of New Jerusalem.

Twelve Tribes: All God's Children

God does not call only sons of Israel His elect; if any Gentile comes into faith, God no more recognizes them as Gentiles but as one belonging in one of the 12 tribes (Romans 2:28-29, 11:13-24). Anyone who has accepted Jesus Christ with faith and received salvation become the descendants of Abraham, the Father of Faith.

Therefore, the '12 tribes of Israel' in spiritual sense refers to 'all the children of God who have been saved by faith'. No matter what the country or race, any child of God who has been saved by faith can take hold of New Jerusalem, the most beautiful place in Heaven.

Each of the 12 tribes of Israel has different characteristics.

In this sense, those souls who go into the city of New Jerusalem will pass through different gates depending on their personal characteristics. It does not mean the magnitude of glory will be different from each other, but only the color and aroma of the glory are different.

Spiritual Meanings in the Names of Twelve Tribes

The spiritual meanings contained in the names of the 12 tribes of Israel have connection with the measure of faith (Romans 12:3) and spiritual growth. Namely, it tells us about the process of sanctifying ourselves to have the qualifications to enter into the city of New Jerusalem, the most beautiful dwelling place of Heaven.

1. Judah: 'Praise'

The name means that we praise the birth of Jesus who came to this earth as the Savior. On the day of His birth, a multitude of heavenly host and angels praised God singing, *"Glory to God in the highest, and on earth peace among men with whom He is pleased"* (Luke 2:14).

2. Reuben: 'Behold the Son'

The first step of Christian faith is to accept Jesus the Son of

God as our personal Savior. We become saved children of God when we accept Jesus Christ.

3. Gad: 'Being Blessed'

Accepting Jesus Christ as our Savior means receiving true blessing that can't be compared with any blessing of this earth. We are blessed because we have been saved by hearing the gospel and having faith in Jesus Christ.

4. Asher: 'Joy'

Once we become the blessed ones by accepting Jesus Christ, we can begin a Christian life that is filled with joy.

5. Naphtali: 'Compete'

Matthew 11:12 says, *"From the days of John the Baptist until now the kingdom of heaven suffers violence, and violent men take it by force."* From this point on, we diligently cast away sins and take hold of heavenly kingdom by force. We gain the hope for better dwelling places in Heaven, and thus we long to take on duties in the church to work for the kingdom of God. We also begin to compete with each other in goodwill and in faith.

6. Manasseh: 'Forget'

As we struggle against and cast away sins while working faithfully for God's kingdom, we reach the 3rd level of faith in which we can practice the words of God. From this stage, even if we have some hard-feelings in certain situations, we do not openly express them. We try to understand in goodness and try to forget the bad aspects of things.

7. Simeon: 'God Hears'

As we go into deeper level in faith having passed each stage, we can go into a stage where God hears us. He searches us and hears our prayers, and He answers us. If we seek, He lets us find; and if we knock, He opens.

8. Levi: 'Uniting'

This means uniting with the Lord and becoming one with Him. Those who truly love the Lord and hope for Heaven will try to be united with the Lord and gradually they will actually become one with Him.

9. Issachar: 'Price'

God lets us reap what we sow and pays us back according to

our actions. It means He gives us different rewards according to our faithfulness and service to His kingdom. This stage also refers to the level where you are faithful until death and try to be faithful in all God's household. And to those who are faithful until death, a crown of life or something better will be given as rewards (Revelation 2:10). Namely, they will be able to go into the third kingdom of heaven or above.

10. Zebulun: 'Dwelling'

If we live in the Word, the truth, light, and goodness completely, we will be able to dwell in New Jerusalem. When we reach this level, John 15:7 will be achieved in our lives, which says, *"If you abide in Me, and My words abide in you, ask whatever you wish, and it will be done for you."*

11. Joseph: Addition

Just as Lot was blessed thanks to his uncle Abraham, if we go into the level of whole spirit, the people around us will also be blessed. We will receive not just what we sow but much more than that.

12. Benjamin: Son of the Right Hand

This means being called a son of God on the right hand side

of God. If we ardently cast away sins, work faithfully for God's kingdom, and become united and one with the Lord, then we can go to New Jerusalem. Furthermore, we will be able to stay close to God's throne and the Lord's throne, living in eternal glory as true sons and daughters of God.

Twelve Steps of Holiness in View of the Names of Twelve Tribes

Complete Holiness
- 12. Benjamin — Being called the son of the right hand
- 11. Joseph — Adding extra blessing in all things
- 10. Zebulun — Dwelling in the truth

Holiness
- 9. Issachar — Receiving the rewards for our faithfulness
- 8. Levi — Being united with the Lord
- 7. Simeon — God hears and answers any prayer
- 6. Manasseh — Forgetting and trying to cast away evil
- 5. Naphtali — Casting away sins and taking hold of Heaven by force
- 4. Asher — Having joy in the heart
- 3. Gad — Receiving the blessing of salvation having accepted the Lord
- 2. Reuben — Becoming God's children having accepted the Lord
- 1. Judah — Praising the birth of the Savior

Measure of Faith: 0 1 2 3 4 5

The Names of the Twelve Apostles on the Twelve Foundations of New Jerusalem

> *"There were three gates on the east and three gates on the north and three gates on the south and three gates on the west. And the wall of the city had twelve foundation stones, and on them were the twelve names of the twelve apostles of the Lamb"* **(Revelation 21:13-14).**

A shadow always reflects the original body. The Old Testament is a shadow and the New Testament the actual body (Hebrews 10:1). The Old Testament talked about Jesus who was to come, and the New Testament writes about the ministry of Jesus who came to this earth and fulfilled the ministry of human salvation.

Similarly, the 12 tribes of the Old Testament is the shadow and the 12 apostles in the New Testament is the body. God taught the apostles through Jesus who fulfilled the Law with love, and let them become the witnesses of the Lord.

The city of New Jerusalem has 12 Pearl Gates, 3 each on the north, south, east, and west wall. There are 12 foundation stones for the walls, and they are adorned with every kind of precious stone. The first foundation stone is jasper; the second, sapphire; the third, chalcedony; the fourth, emerald; the fifth, sardonyx; the sixth, sardius; the seventh, chrysolite; the eighth, beryl; the ninth, topaz; the tenth, chrysoprase; the eleventh, jacinth; the twelfth, amethyst (Revelation 21:19-20).

On top of these precious stones are written the names of the 12 apostles of Jesus. Of course, the name of Judas Iscariot is not there because he betrayed Jesus.

The Spiritual Meaning of the Twelve Apostles

In Acts chapter 1, after the resurrected Lord ascended into heaven, the disciples focused on prayer in Jerusalem. Then they elected a person to replace Judas Iscariot. He was selected among those who were taught by Jesus, and he is Mathias.

This event represents two meanings. First, it is that not only the elect but the Gentiles could also receive salvation. Second, it means anyone can be chosen like Mathias if they are united with the Lord.

The 12 apostles spiritually represent 'those who are holy and have been faithful in all God's household'. If anyone accepts Jesus Christ with faith, and then struggle against sins to the point of shedding blood to achieve holiness and fulfill all their God-given duties completely, they can go into the city of New Jerusalem, which is the most beautiful dwelling place in the kingdom of heaven.

The Author
Dr. Jaerock Lee

Dr. Jaerock Lee was born in Muan, Jeonnam Province, Republic of Korea, in 1943. While in his twenties, Dr. Lee suffered from a variety of incurable diseases for seven years and awaited death with no hope for recovery. However one day in the spring of 1974 he was led to a church by his sister, and when he knelt down to pray, the living God immediately healed him of all his diseases.

From the moment he met the living God through that wonderful experience, Dr. Lee has loved God with all his heart and sincerity, and in 1978 he was called to be a servant of God. He prayed fervently with countless fasting prayers so that he could clearly understand the will of God, wholly accomplish it and obey the Word of God. In 1982, he founded Manmin Central Church in Seoul, South Korea, and countless works of God, including miraculous healings, signs and wonders, have been taking place at his church ever since.

In 1986, Dr. Lee was ordained as a pastor at the Annual Assembly of Jesus' Sungkyul(Holiness) Church of Korea, and four years later in 1990, his sermons began to be broadcast in Australia, Russia, and the Philippines. Within a short time many more countries were being reached through the Far East Broadcasting Company, the Asia Broadcast Station, and the Washington Christian Radio System.

Three years later, in 1993, Manmin Central Church was selected as one of the "World's Top 50 Churches" by the *Christian World* magazine (US) and he received an Honorary Doctorate of Divinity from Christian Faith College, Florida, USA, and in 1996 he received his Ph. D. in Ministry from Kingsway Theological Seminary, Iowa, USA.

Since 1993, Dr. Lee has been spearheading world evangelization through many overseas crusades in Tanzania, Argentina, L.A., Baltimore City, Hawaii, and New York City of the USA, Uganda, Japan, Pakistan, Kenya, the Philippines, Honduras, India, Russia, Germany, Peru, Democratic Republic of the Congo, Israel and Estonia.

In 2002 he was acknowledged as a "worldwide revivalist" for his powerful ministries in various overseas crusades by major Christian newspapers in Korea. In particular was his 'New York Crusade 2006' held in Madison Square Garden, the most famous arena in the world. The event was broadcast to 220 nations, and in his 'Israel United Crusade 2009', held at the International Convention Center (ICC) in Jerusalem he boldly proclaimed Jesus Christ is the Messiah and Savior.

His sermons are broadcast to 176 nations via satellites including GCN TV and he was listed as one of the 'Top 10 Most Influential Christian Leaders' of 2009 and 2010 by the popular Russian Christian magazine *In Victory* and news agency *Christian Telegraph* for his powerful TV broadcasting ministry and overseas church-pastoring ministry.

As of June of 2018, Manmin Central Church has a congregation of more than 130,000 members. There are 11,000 branch churches world-wide including 56 domestic branch churches, and more than 100 missionaries have been commissioned to 26 countries, including the United States, Russia, Germany, Canada, Japan, China, France, India, Kenya, and many more so far.

As of the date of this publishing, Dr. Lee has written 112 books, including bestsellers *Tasting Eternal Life before Death, My Life My Faith I & II, The Message of the Cross, The Measure of Faith, Heaven I & II, Hell, Awaken Israel!*, and *The Power of God*. His works have been translated into more than 76 languages.

His Christian columns appear on *The Hankook Ilbo, The JoongAng Daily, The Chosun Ilbo, The Dong-A Ilbo, The Hankyoreh Shinmun, The Seoul Shinmun, The Kyunghyang Shinmun, The Korea Economic Daily, The Shisa News,* and *The Christian Press.*

Dr. Lee is currently leader of many missionary organizations and associations. Positions include: Chairman, The United Holiness Church of Jesus Christ; Permanent President, The World Christianity Revival Mission Association; Founder & Board Chairman, Global Christian Network (GCN); Founder & Board Chairman, World Christian Doctors Network (WCDN); and Founder & Board Chairman, Manmin International Seminary (MIS).

Other powerful books by the same author

Heaven I & II

A detailed sketch of the gorgeous living environment the heavenly citizens enjoy and beautiful description of different levels of heavenly kingdoms.

Tasting Eternal Life Before Death

A testimonial memoirs of Dr. Jaerock Lee, who was born again and saved from the valley of the shadow of death and has been leading a perfect exemplary Christian life.

Hell

An earnest message to all mankind from God, who wishes not even one soul to fall into the depths of hell! You will discover the never-before-revealed account of the cruel reality of the Lower Grave and Hell.

My Life My Faith I & II

Dr. Jaerock Lee's autobiography provides the most fragrant spiritual aroma for the readers, through his life extracted from the love of God blossomed in midst of the dark waves, cold yoke and the deepest despair.

The Measure of Faith

What kind of a dwelling place, crown and reward are prepared for you in heaven? This book provides with wisdom and guidance for you to measure your faith and cultivate the best and most mature faith.

Spirit, Soul, and Body I & II

A guidebook that gives the reader spiritual understanding of spirit, soul, and body, and helps him find what kind of 'self' he has made so that he can gain the power to defeat darkness and become a person of spirit.

Awaken, Israel

Why has God kept His eyes on Israel from the beginning of the world to this day? What kind of His providence has been prepared for Israel in the last days, who await the Messiah?

Seven Churches

The Lord's earnest messages awakening believers and churches from spiritual slumber, sent to the seven churches recorded in Revelation chapter 2 and 3, which refer to all the churches of the Lord

Footsteps of the Lord I & II

An unraveled account of secrets about the beginning of time, the origin of Jesus, and God's providence and love for allowing His only begotten Son Passion and resurrection!

The Power of God

This is a 'must-read' that serves as an essential guide by which one can possess true faith and experience the wondrous power of God

www.urimbooks.com

Confessions

God clearly let me know His endless heart and will that is contained in the Bible. He also let me know the confessions that God, the Lord, and the patriarchs of faith made from their hearts.

Against Such Things There Is No Law

As they bear the fruits of the Holy Spirit, Christians gain true freedom and can check themselves as to how sanctified they are, how close they can get to God's throne, and as to how much they have cultivated the heart of the Lord

Love: Fulfillment of the Law

Spiritual love is to love the other person with an unchanging heart not desiring anything in return; however, fleshly love changes in different situations and circumstances. This book guides readers to possess spiritual love that is precious and beautiful.

A Man Who Pursues True Blessing

Jesus' message titled "Beatitudes" helps us realize what true blessing is so that we will not only enjoy all the blessings of this world including wealth, health, fame, and authority, but possess New Jerusalem.

Lectures on the First Corinthians I & II

A 'basics' guidebook for Christian accounting and ways to resolve various life problems including lawsuits, strife, marriage, idolatry, and the spiritual gifts and for the victory in spiritual warfare.

www.urimbooks.com

www.ingramcontent.com/pod-product-compliance
Lightning Source LLC
LaVergne TN
LVHW041223080526
838199LV00083B/2405